Heir to the Sooner Legacy

THE CHAMPIONSHIP STORY OF OKLAHOMA COACH BOB STOOPS

AN EPIC SPORTS BOOK

THE OKLAHOMAN
oklahoman.com

THE OKLAHOMAN
oklahoman.com

EDWARD L. GAYLORD, CHAIRMAN AND PUBLISHER
E.K. GAYLORD II, PRESIDENT
EDMUND O. MARTIN, VICE PRESIDENT AND GENERAL MANAGER
CHRISTY GAYLORD EVEREST, VICE PRESIDENT
SUE A. HALE, EXECUTIVE EDITOR
BOB COLON, EXECUTIVE SPORTS EDITOR
BERRY TRAMEL, SPORTS EDITOR
JAMES ARGO, PHOTO EDITOR
DICK DUGAN, PROMOTIONS MANAGER

Acknowledgments: Joe Hight, Managing Editor/Sports; Mike Koehler, Deputy Sports Editor; George Wilson, Director of Photo Technology, and *The Daily Oklahoman* Sports, Photo, News and Promotion Departments.

Cover and book design: Kathy Sellers, Communication Arts, Birmingham, Ala.
Published by: Epic Sports, Birmingham, Ala.

PHOTO CREDITS:

Jaconna Aguirre: *PG-8 (top).*
Jim Beckel: *PG-12 (top).*
Steve Gooch: *PG-8 (bottom),*
    PG-15 (top right).
Paul Hellstern: *PG-9 (top).*
Doug Hoke: *Front Cover, Back Cover*
    (bottom left), PG-5 (bottom), PG-6,
    PG-11, PG-13, PG-15 (bottom).
Iowa University Athletic Dept.:
    PG-2 (both), PG-3.

Kansas State University
    Athletic Dept.: *PG-4 (top).*
Ty Russell: *PG-10, PG-16 (both).*
Steve Sisney: *Back Cover (right),*
    PG-7, PG-12 (bottom), PG-14
    (both), PG-15 (top left).
Bryan Terry: *Back Cover (top left),*
    PG-9 (bottom).
The Oklahoman Archives:
    PG-1 (all), PG-5 (top).
University of Florida
    Athletic Dept.: *PG-4 (bottom).*

INTRODUCTION

Oklahoma is the land of opportunity.

This patch of land, carved from the middle of the country and developed later than all the territories surrounding it, has provided opportunity for two centuries.

Indians were sent here to die in the 1830's, yet instead they built great civilizations. Men long on dreams and short on cash came here for land in the 1890's. Entrepreneurs arrived in the early part of the 20th century for a new commodity called oil.

And since World War II, Oklahoma has provided a chance for another kind of dreamer, another kind of man who sniffed opportunity sifting out of the red clay.

Football coaches.

Since WWII, three men with no Oklahoma ties journeyed to our state seeking football success and forged it almost immediately.

Bud Wilkinson. Barry Switzer. Bob Stoops.

Wilkinson arrived in 1946, became OU's head coach in 1947, won a national title by 1950 and soon was a legend.

Switzer arrived in 1966, became OU's head coach in 1973, won a national title by 1974 and soon was a folk hero.

Stoops arrived in 1999 as OU's head coach, won a national title by 2000 and has no limits on how high he can rise in the psyche of Oklahomans.

Wilkinson, Switzer and Stoops — they were more different than alike. The stately Wilkinson; cerebral, studious, almost holy. The earthy Switzer; funny, honest, charming. The self-assured Stoops; confident, matter of fact, street smart.

But they shared two common traits: both coached butt-kicking football teams that became America's best, and both had that certain something that makes leaders of men. You don't know how to describe it, but you know it when you see it.

And just like with Wilkinson and Switzer, all who meet Stoops come away impressed with the qualities of the man. A man born to

3

coach football, a man born to lead.

This book, culled from the pages of The Daily Oklahoman, goes in-depth to reveal just who is this man and how he captured a state. From his upbringing in Youngstown, Ohio; to his coaching odyssey through Iowa and Kent State and Kansas State and Florida; to his arrival in Norman, where after 25 games he's become the nation's hottest coach.

Bob Stoops came to Oklahoma and, like many before him, seized opportunity. He is a worthy heir to the legacy of Bud Wilkinson and Barry Switzer.

Berry Tramel
Sports Editor, The Daily Oklahoman

CONTENTS

A CHAMPIONS' SCRAPBOOK

THE 1999 SEASON

The 2000 Season

A
CHAMPIONS'
SCRAPBOOK

GATOR AIDE STOOPS COULD BE PERFECT FIT FOR OU

By Dave Sittler
The Daily Oklahoman, Oct. 28, 1998

A REPORT surfaced this week that Florida defensive coordinator Bob Stoops had preliminary discussions with Oklahoma about his interest in becoming the Sooners' next head coach.

Stoops did not return telephone messages left Tuesday at his Gainesville, Fla., office. OU athletic director Joe Castiglione said no one associated with the university has talked to Stoops or any coach because the Sooners don't have an opening.

OU will have an opening by Nov. 23. And the more one studies Stoops' resume, it becomes obvious that the 38-year-old Gators' assistant should be on the shortest of OU's short list.

Key OU insiders have confirmed if John Blake is either fired or reassigned, the school will move quickly to hire his successor. Because of recruiting, the Sooners want a new coach on board less than two weeks after the final game on Nov. 21 against Texas Tech.

It would be difficult to convince a head coach from a bowl-bound team — like Georgia's Jim Donnan or Tulane's Tommy Bowden — to leave before the bowl game. Mack Brown did it last year when he left North Carolina for Texas before the Tar Heels defeated Virginia Tech in the Gator Bowl. Most head coaches would allow an assistant to leave early if it were a step up in the profession. But the time factor isn't the only thing that has made the smart, charismatic Stoops the hottest candidate among Division I-A assistants.

He's worked wonders with Florida's defense. The year he took over, 1996, the Gators won the national championship. No wonder Florida coach Steve Spurrier pays him a total package worth more than $200,000 a year.

"I think he'll be a head coach within one, two or three years," Spurrier told The Gainesville Sun. "There will be an opportunity soon that he will probably go for."

Some observers believe Stoops will wait for Iowa coach Hayden Fry to retire so he can return to the school where he was a four-year starter and All-American defensive back in 1982. Others believe Stoops knows that Iowa defensive coordinator Bob Elliott is the man Fry has selected as his eventual replacement.

"That's (Iowa) a place that always will be warm in my heart," Stoops told reporters last summer. "But I'm also smart enough to know there will be many people who will want that job when it becomes available."

In addition to his defensive knowledge, organizational skills and reputation as an excellent recruiter, Stoops is attractive to OU because of his ties to the old Big Eight Conference. Stoops worked for Bill Snyder, the genius who pulled off the "Manhattan Miracle" at Kansas State.

A part of Snyder's original K-State staff, Stoops has hands-on experience when it comes to rebuilding a program. And OU certainly isn't anywhere near as bad off as what Snyder and Stoops found when they arrived at K-State in 1989.

Stoops' defensive philosophy is similar to what OU runs this season. It's an attacking, blitzing style built on speed and pressing receivers with aggressive man-to-man coverage. Spurrier has so much confidence in Stoops that he doesn't spend any time coaching the defense.

"What coach Spurrier is to the offense, Coach Stoops is to the defense," Gator cornerback Tony George said. "You love to play for guys like Coach Stoops. He's a great friend and person outside of football as well. Knowing he's on your side is a great feeling."

Several schools have wanted Stoops on their side. Two years ago, Stoops turned down a seven-year, $3 million offer from Minnesota because he didn't feel the school was committed to winning. A year ago, he declined a chance to interview at Arkansas. When Brown got the Texas job, he reportedly offered Stoops a whopping salary to coach the defense.

"I want to be a head coach and I feel I'm prepared for it," Stoops said before the start of this season. "I want it to be the right time and the right place ... a place that fits."

In less than a month, Stoops could be the right man and the perfect fit at a place called Oklahoma.

OU TURNS TO STOOPS TO TAKE FOOTBALL REINS

By Jim Killackey and Mac Bentley
The Daily Oklahoman, Dec. 1, 1998

Norman — Bob Stoops — "the brightest young rising star in college football" — is the man University of Oklahoma officials believe will return the Sooners to glory, grandeur and championships.

Stoops, defensive coordinator, will be introduced today to an expectant and victory-hungry throng as OU's 21st head football coach. Stoops is expected to attend the afternoon announcement and news conference.

He accepted what is expected to be a five-year deal worth at least $700,000 a year.

Stoops was OU's first choice from the outset of a seven-day search to replace John Blake. He was the only candidate interviewed face to face by OU Athletic Director Joe Castiglione, university officials said.

"Bob Stoops is a great fit for the University of Oklahoma," said OU regent Stephen F. Bentley, who was among the officials who interviewed Stoops.

During a nearly eight-hour meeting Sunday in Dallas, Stoops

12

met with Castiglione, OU President David Boren, three OU regents, Chuck Neinas and Eddie Crowder.

Neinas, the former Big Eight Conference commissioner and executive director of the College Football Association, is now a Colorado-based consultant for athletic departments. Crowder, former head coach at the University of Colorado, was a quarterback at OU in the 1950's under legendary coach Bud Wilkinson.

Crowder, reached at his Colorado home Monday evening, deferred comment until the university made an official announcement.

"I don't know for sure," he said when asked how he became involved in the selection process. "I was called, just asked to be a minor participant."

Neinas, considered by some the No. 1 expert in the recruitment of college coaches, was paid a fee by Castiglione to help with the search.

Former OU all-American Lee Roy Selmon, now an associate athletic director at the University of South Florida in Tampa, Fla., also played a key role in Stoops' selection.

"Everybody that I talked to said he was an outstanding person and felt he could do a good job as a head coach," Selmon said Monday night.

Stoops, a Florida assistant coach in Gainesville, Fla., and former assistant at Kansas State University, will have his contract approved during a regularly scheduled OU regents' meeting Dec. 9 in Norman.

"We determined that Bob Stoops is the brightest young rising star in college football," a highly placed OU official told The Oklahoman on Monday.

"Bob has been a first-hand participant in winning football programs and he knows what it takes to be victorious. He knows the kind of pressure involved in high-caliber championship football.

"It was better to take a top assistant at a top program" than an older head coach elsewhere, the source said.

Stoops was "very sought-after" and "has no skeletons in the closet" that could hinder his tenure, the source said.

"We had great reports on him," the source said.

The three university regents who met Stoops at a hotel near a Dallas airport Sunday did not include Chairman Melvin C. Hall, a staunch supporter of fired coach Blake.

Stoops, 38, replaces Blake, who was 34 when he was hired in December 1995. Blake compiled a 12-22 record in three seasons. He was fired Nov. 22.

The University of Florida Gators were 9-2 this season and will be playing in an as-yet undetermined bowl game.

Stoops played and coached at the University of Iowa in Iowa City, Iowa, and was co-defensive coordinator at Kansas State before joining the Gators, where he was the assistant head coach, defensive coordinator and secondary coach.

At Florida, Stoops added the defensive punch to go with head coach Steve Spurrier's genius on offense. In his first season, the combination produced a national championship.

Stoops' defensive teams have been ranked among the nation's Top 20 during each of his three seasons there.

OU has six national championships but has not had a winning season since 1993. The Sooners have gone 23-33-1 in the past five years under Gary Gibbs, Howard Schnellenberger and Blake.

STOOPS HAS COMMON LINK TO OU GREATS

By Berry Tramel
The Daily Oklahoman, Dec. 1, 1998

Bᴉʟʟ Sɴʏᴅᴇʀ calls him Bobby. Steve Spurrier calls him Stoopsie. Hayden Fry calls him to take over his office.

You can call him qualified.

Bob Stoops is the 21st head coach in Oklahoma Sooner history. Almost all were ready to take command, but none more so than this 38-year-old defensive whiz from the football country of Youngstown, Ohio.

Fry. Snyder. Spurrier.

Stoops has worked and/or played for the nation's best program builders. Chief lieutenant, assistant head coach, for Snyder and Spurrier. Played and coached for Fry.

Kansas State, Florida, Iowa. Maybe the three best building jobs in college football the last 20 years. Snyder has made K-State the ultimate Cinderella. Spurrier has made Florida a monster. Fry made Iowa a Rose Bowl contender after 18 straight losing seasons.

They have a common link. All wanted Bob Stoops on their sideline; Fry made him a graduate assistant at age 22, and Snyder and Spurrier made him chief lieutenant.

15

And so Stoops has a common link with the best coaches in OU history. Just like Bud Wilkinson, Barry Switzer and Chuck Fairbanks, his first head coaching job was in Norman. Just like Wilkinson, Switzer and Fairbanks, he learned at the feet of masters.

Wilkinson coached for Ossie Solem at Syracuse, the legendary Don Faurot for Iowa Pre-Flight and the bigger-than-life Jim Tatum at OU.

Switzer coached for Frank Broyles at Arkansas and Jim Mackenzie and Fairbanks at OU.

And Fairbanks coached for Duffy Daugherty at Michigan State, Frank Kush at Arizona State, Bill Yeoman at Houston and Mackenzie. That's a list almost as impressive as Snyder, Spurrier and Fry.

Hiring assistants to be head coaches can be risky. Check out Gomer Jones and John Blake. But so can hiring head coaches. Howard Schnellenberger comes to mind.

It's hard to imagine an assistant better prepared than Stoops; 38 years old, phenomenal success at multiple stops, smart enough to wait on a big-time program to call.

So forget the concern of hiring an assistant. And for that matter, quit worrying about hiring another defensive guy.

In the last nine years, OU has had only one season with an offense-groomed head coach, Schnellenberger in 1995. Gary Gibbs was defense. John Blake was defense. Guilt by association.

In December 1998, Oklahoma needs one thing and one thing only: a good coach. Young or old, head or assistant, offense or defense, right-handed or left-handed, doesn't matter. As long as he's good .

And Stoops appears to be good. Frankly, throw out the connection with Spurrier and Fry, and Stoops remains college football's top young gun. Anyone who sniffed the same air as Bill Snyder seems qualified, and Stoops was one of the main men of the Manhattan Miracle.

After his practice on Monday in Manhattan, Kan., Snyder said, "I am very proud of and happy for Bobby, and pleased with (OU athletic director) Joe Castiglione for his insight in the hiring process.

"Bobby has all the traits necessary to become a very successful head coach, along with some great experiences with several very fine football programs. He will do very well at the University of Oklahoma."

Stoops' history agrees. So does OU's.

OU BEGINS THE STOOPS ERA, NEW COACH STATES HIS GOAL: WIN

By John Rohde
The Daily Oklahoman, Dec. 2, 1998

NORMAN — Making no promises and proclaiming his program will regroup rather than rebuild, a confident Bob Stoops was introduced as Oklahoma's 21st football coach Tuesday afternoon.

"I'm not going to come in with a bunch of promises and say, 'Hey, we're going to win this year or that year,' or how many (games) we're going to win," Stoops said. "I believe you go into every game trying to win, and we're going to do that. If I were to say we expect to be 9-2 next year, that means I'm giving up two games."

Roughly 1,000 people gathered for the announcement, held outside on the front porch of Evans Hall on the north oval.

It will be the first head-coaching position for the 38-year-old Stoops, who served as defensive coordinator at Florida the last three seasons. Before that, Stoops spent seven seasons as an assistant while helping Kansas State make one of the most remarkable turnarounds in college football history.

Stoops played defensive back at Iowa, where he later served as a

18

volunteer and graduate assistant from 1983-87. From there, he spent one season as an assistant at Kent State before joining the Kansas State staff in 1989.

With strong ties still at Iowa, many Hawkeyes supporters believed Stoops would succeed long-time coach Hayden Fry, for whom Stoops played from 1979-82.

Stoops, however, said he was never torn between Iowa and Oklahoma.

"No. You cannot allow it," Stoops said. "That's a business decision to do what you feel is best for your family. You look at the potential here at Oklahoma and what we can do with this program ... all (of which) made this an easy decision. I've never compared (the OU job) to other jobs. I've had opportunities with other schools, not just Iowa. This has always been the one that I've had my eye on for a long time, wondering if I'd ever be in the position to have a chance at it."

Oklahoma athletic director Joe Castiglione served as a one-man search committee to fill a position that became vacant with the firing of John Blake on Nov. 22.

The Sooners have not had a winning season in six years.

OU went 12-22 in three seasons under Blake. Before that, the Sooners were 5-5-1 in one season under Howard Schnellenberger and 6-6 in their final year under Gary Gibbs.

Stoops said he longed for the Oklahoma job because of the program's storied tradition and high expectations.

"People are going to expect what they want," Stoops said. "Certainly, I expect more. I expect us to be in a position next year to be very good, to have a chance to win many games, if not all of them."

Although he has never been a head coach, Stoops comes from a strong pedigree, having served alongside Fry, Steve Spurrier at Florida, Bill Snyder at Kansas State, Wisconsin coach Barry Alvarez (at Iowa) and Iowa State coach Dan McCarney (at Iowa).

Asked if any aspect of the OU job overwhelms or intimidates him, Stoops said: "I don't believe it does. I believe I've been extremely fortunate to be with the people I've been with. There's been tremendous coaches I've been around.

"Being with Bill Snyder for seven years, rebuilding the program there, I couldn't get any better experience. Being with Steve Spurrier the last three years has been an amazing experience, to handle the big games, the national championship games. I believe where I've been has given me great preparation to be able to handle the (OU) position."

Stoops said he soon will begin his search for assistant coaches.

"It'll start fairly quick, in the next two or three days," he said. "That's going to be an ongoing process. I expect to have some on board next week."

After addressing the public and the media, Stoops met with OU players.

"I hope to gain their trust and respect by being around them," said Stoops, who also telephoned recruits Tuesday night.

As for convincing people he warrants being the Sooners' coach, Stoops said: "I'm not going to sit here and try to sway anyone's opinion. They feel how they feel. I'm sure there were some young head coaches who would have been qualified. All I can say is I certainly feel very comfortable in the position.

"I feel I can attract and get the staff that will be strong and knows how to win. I believe in time that I'll be a guy they'll be happy with. For me to try and change anyone's opinion today, it's not going to happen, so I won't try to."

OU MAKING STRIDES UNDER STOOPS' REIGN

By Berry Tramel
The Daily Oklahoman, Jan. 17, 1999

NORMAN — Bob Stoops knew Oklahoma was meant to be his new home during a two-hour stretch of big news a couple of weeks ago.

During a recruiting dead period, Stoops was back in Gainesville, Fla., with his wife. They were told their offer on a house in Norman had been accepted. Then in a doctor's office waiting room came the call telling them their Florida home had sold.

Finally, in they went to see the doctor, who had quite a diagnosis: Carol Stoops is pregnant with twins, due in July.

"I said, 'This was meant to be,'" Stoops said Tuesday from his sparkling, but unfinished, new office in the Barry Switzer Center.

Anyone who has crossed paths with Stoops would agree. In 47 days on the job, he is winning friends and inspiring confidence with a down-to-Earth, we'll-get-it-done demeanor.

No bluster, no airs. Stoops is confident yet unpretentious. He seems to talk to the carpenter working on his office the same way he talks to staff members.

Stoops is winning over OU personnel with a considerate, genuine personality.

Example: One day he walked into the athletic mess hall, grabbed a tray of lunch, sat down and introduced himself to long-time assistant track coach Pete Kron, who had been dining alone.

Stoops appears to be the best kind of big man on campus: He doesn't act like it.

"People have been wonderful," Stoops said, referring to the people he's working with and the letters he's received and the fans who have stopped him on the street.

Ironically, the slowest reception has come from the group that matters most in the next two weeks: high school seniors. OU entered the weekend with just four known commitments. Archrivals Texas and Oklahoma State have been in double digits since December.

Hired on Dec. 1, Stoops got a late start. He admits that.

He also takes over a Sooner program at its lowest point in what, 55 years? 75 years? 95 years? He doesn't admit that.

"That has nothing to do with now. I don't even recognize that," Stoops said. "It's not something I want to talk about or bring up. We're just looking ahead to meeting our expectations."

Stoops talks plain and simple. That doesn't mean he's different from every football coach when it comes to recruiting talk. Going great. Making inroads. Weekend went very well. Stoops used all the cliches.

But he did warn fans to be careful of what they read on the Internet or hear on the radio. The Internet, he said, "is as wrong as often as it is right." And recruits these days know how to play the game; they know what to tell reporters to get their names built up.

"People just have to be very wary what they read, what they hear, because so often it isn't accurate," Stoops said.

Stoops said the new Switzer Center is impressive to recruits and that OU's academic center is always a hit.

But isn't the lack of commitments a concern?

"What are you going to do about it?" he said. "We're certainly not going to have 16 when we don't have a staff here. Why be alarmed about something you have no control over?

"We're going to take pride in recruiting the best players we can find. The bottom line is watching tape, evaluating, finding players you believe make your team better. Whether someone's recruiting them or not has nothing to do with anything."

Stoops said Oklahoma remains a great football school, even if teenagers don't realize it right off. "The more they talk with you, they realize it," he said. "Certainly their parents always do."

Stoops' staff is complete, and he's dropping more and more hints about his philosophy. He didn't commit the day he was hired, but it seems certain now that the Sooners will try to head off opponents with the pass.

He hired Kentucky offensive coordinator Mike Leach. He signed a throwing junior-college quarterback, Josh Heupel. He is talking more and more about his offensive tendencies.

"You've got to throw the football," he said bluntly. "If you really pay attention to how teams move the football these days ... it's a proven system, not just at Kentucky."

He likes to tell the story of coaching against Kentucky in 1996, the year before Leach and head coach Hal Mumme got to UK. Stoops' Florida defense held Kentucky to 68 yards, four first downs and no points. The next year, UK went for almost 500 total yards, 153 of it rushing, 28 points and 25 first downs.

"With the same people," Stoops said, although in the meantime Tim Couch did grow from a freshman to a sophomore. "What's different? It's the system.

"It's a system that's fun to watch and gives them a chance to make plays."

Soon recruiting will end, and Stoops' new life will find its normalcy. His new staff, which has been all together just once before this weekend, will settle into a routine. His family — Carol and 2-year-old daughter Mackenzie — will move to town in February.

And Stoops can start settling into a position (head coach) he had never held in a place (Oklahoma) he had never lived.

"I felt, in all honesty, comfortable right away," he said. "Certainly being familiar with the area, getting to know people, takes a little more time."

A little more time. That might be the only time Stoops uses that phrase. He doesn't claim to need time to resurrect Sooner football. He thinks OU should win and win now.

"You hear guys say, I need four years," Stoops said. "All they're doing is giving themselves a cushion. You'll never hear me say something like that."

There he goes again, winning friends and inspiring confidence.

SOONERS HAVE STOOPS BUT LITTLE TALENT

By Berry Tramel
The Daily Oklahoman, July 4, 1999

T HE QUESTION was loaded and dang it, Bob Stoops wouldn't bite.

Looks like he's never going to. The new Oklahoma football coach is pretty sharp — or stubborn, which isn't necessarily a bad thing. Either way, he's like a tree that's planted by the waters. Immovable.

Is there enough talent on campus to win?

Ouch. A swipe at Stoops with a two-edged sword. Admit there's no talent, and he's making excuses, a capital crime in Stoopsville. Claim there is talent, and he's fibbing, which is never a good idea in any 'ville.

Stoops wants no part of the loaded question, which of course is rhetorical. Heck no, there's not enough talent on campus to win. Great football players stopped showing up in Norman long ago. Good football players are in short supply.

Sure, the Sooners under John Blake were underachievers and undercoached. But more than that, they were overmatched.

You don't get beat 51-7 and 73-21 and 38-7 because the wrong play was called. You don't get beat that bad in crimson and cream only because of who is wearing the headsets. You get beat that bad because of who is wearing the helmets.

Yes, Stoops is a huge upgrade on the Sooner sidelines. Yes, hope, real hope, is back. But the winning won't return until the talent does.

Quick, scan the OU roster and who gets you excited about autumn? OK, the Stoops brothers and their track record of championship defense. Pass-happy offensive coordinator Mike Leach.

But players? The Woodses, Mike and Pee Wee, are OK senior cornerbacks. Jarrail Jackson is a big-time punt returner. Rocky Calmus looked good as a freshman linebacker. There are some decent veteran defensive linemen.

Not exactly 1975. Not exactly 1995. The list is short. Look at it this way: OU handed over its quarterback reins to a junior college transfer. Josh Heupel could turn out to be the real deal, but you want juco players to earn a job. By necessity, Heupel had to step in uncontested.

Sooner recruiting basically has been sliding for years. OU has had only one All-Big 12 player per year since the conference formed: Kelly Gregg in '98, DeMond Parker in '97 and Tyrell Peters in '96. OU hasn't had a first-round draft pick since Cedric Jones in '95, and in the last three NFL drafts only two Sooners were selected before the fifth round.

As retired Del City coach Henry Manning liked to say, "It's not the X's and the O's, it's the Johnnies and the Joes."

Put down the band-aids, Doctor Stoops. This is a program that needs a transplant surgeon.

Just don't expect Stoops to admit it. Excuses have been cast from his kingdom, he said the December day he was hired. No excuses, he's said ever since. This is Oklahoma. Oklahoma should win. That's what a million Oklahomans have been screaming into the prairie wind for a long time.

No excuses, even when the best football excuse — no talent — is available.

"Our players are going to understand from us that we believe in them, that they should believe in us," Stoops said. "You're never going to hear out of my mouth that our players don't have talent."

His lieutenants, Leach and Mike Stoops, follow in line.

"Our expectations are as high as everybody's," Leach said. "If we have a few guys step up, do a good job of coaching, I think we'll be pretty good."

Courageous talk. But frankly, Stoops has inherited a rag-tag team. Offensive players recruited for a system totally foreign to what the Sooners will run. Defenders who played over their head for Rex Ryan last season and now have to abandon the 46 philosophy they took to so well.

Bob Stoops did admit that more talent is always needed anywhere at anytime but said not only will recruiting be upgraded, current talent will be developed. More strength, more speed, more depth.

"I believe we do have a good group," Stoops said.

I don't. There is no reason why Stoops' first OU team should win. Except for a coach who says losing is not an option.

A NEW SHERIFF IN TOWN

By Mac Bentley
The Daily Oklahoman, Aug. 29, 1999

B OB STOOPS appears to have been dealt a better hand than John Blake, but not nearly so pat as the one Howard Schnellenberger received.

Stoops is the third coach in five years hired by the University of Oklahoma in its effort to restore the Sooner football program to its former stature.

It's a program that won its sixth and most recent national championship in 1985 and its 33rd and most recent conference championship in 1987. It's a program that hasn't won as many as 10 games in a season since. A program that has won just 42 of 80 conference games since. And a program that is 10-21 inside the conference over the past four years.

On paper, at least, it appears Stoops is better-armed to lead the Sooners to their first winning regular season since 1994 than was Blake when he took over in 1996. OU's immediate future is not nearly so bright as it was when Schnellenberger assumed command in 1995, though.

Schnellenberger has been ridiculed by media and fans alike for his prophecies of conference and national championships, but from a 1999 perspective, he had every reason to be cocksure.

He inherited a team that was coming off a 6-5 regular season, 4-3 in the Big Eight, and a humiliating, 31-6 loss to Brigham Young in the Copper Bowl. Schnellenberger inherited 54 lettermen, a whopping 19 starters and 20 other players who had started at least one game.

That 1995 team included five starters who were already or would be first-team all-conference selections, including 1994 All-Big Eight performers Cedric Jones and Darrius Johnson, and it included six players who would be taken in the NFL draft.

Oh, what a waste. After opening the season 3-0, that team went 2-5-1 and didn't even score a point in its last 2 $\frac{1}{2}$ games. One can only wonder if that season pushed the Sooners over the cliff, or if the downward momentum was already too strong to stop.

Blake inherited nine returning starters in 1996, the fewest at OU since the 3-7, 1965 team, and debuted with a 3-8 record, 3-5 in the Big 12.

Stoops begins his first season with 38 lettermen and 15 starters from last year's 5-6, 3-5 team, but no returning all-conference players. Unlike Schnellenberger, he hasn't predicted book and movie deals, and unlike Blake, he hasn't said it will take a few years to reinvent the program.

"We expect to be good and expect to be in every game and expect to win a bunch of football games," he said. "Some people ask me how I can say that ... 'don't you want to tell everyone not to expect too much?'

"I don't believe in that; I believe we do have a good nucleus of players that we've got a good chance to win with. If I told our players it's going to take us four or five years to win, they might believe me and it might take that long. I hope that's not the case."

The Sooners return a ton of experience on the offensive line with the likes of Scott Kempenich, Jay Smith, Adam Carpenter, Matt O'Neal, Bubba Burcham, Jason Bronson and Stockar McDougle. That group is joined by former defensive lineman Ryan Allen.

Jarrail Jackson returns at wide receiver, where the Sooners were hit hard by graduation but appear to have recovered nicely with

Andre Woolfolk, Curtis Fagan, DaWight Benning, Damien Mackey and Mike Jackson.

Fullback Seth Littrell is a returning starter at the H-back position, and the Sooners, despite the loss of Jason Freeman, will again be well-represented at tight end by Matt Anderson, Chris Hammons and Trent Smith.

Inconsistent play at quarterback could be a thing of the past with the addition of juco transfer Josh Heupel, who it would seem was born to run offensive coordinator Mike Leach's multiple offense.

"I don't believe in this day and age that you're able to win without throwing the football," said Stoops. "You look at Tennessee winning a national championship, had a lot of big plays passing. Look at A&M in the championship game against Kansas State, to win the game they threw a pass that went for a touch.

"Anymore, teams that win are the teams that are balanced, can do both. We intend to be a balanced offense that can do both, run and pass and keep people off-balance and hopefully take advantage of what they're trying to take away. You've got to be able to do both."

The Sooners likely will pass the ball more than they run it, but it's a controlled passing game that will involve running backs as much as the receivers.

On defense, the front four will be experienced with the likes of Frank Romero, Bary Holleyman, Corey Callens, Cornelius Burton, Rocky Bright, Jeremy Wilson-Guest, Greg Muhammad and Ryan Fisher, and will get some help from juco transfer Ramon Richardson.

More juco help comes at linebacker in the form of Torrence Marshall, who joins returning performers Brandon Moore, Rocky Calmus, Nick Simpson and Armand Spence.

The Sooner coaches are high on the secondary with returning performers Mike Woods, Rodney Rideau, Ontei Jones, Pee Wee Woods and William Bartee. Help could come from first-year players Michael Thompson and Derrick Strait.

That's pretty much the cast that will be trying to reverse a trend that has seen the Sooners go 2-5-1 against Texas and Oklahoma State over the past four years. OU is also 0-3 against Nebraska during that time, but the Sooners don't play the Cornhuskers this season. Unless ... well, there is that Dec. 4 Big 12 championship game.

"Stranger things have happened," Stoops said.

OU

SHOW GOES ON UNDER STOOPS' BIG TOP

By Dave Sittler
The Daily Oklahoman, Oct. 13, 1999

F ROM BANDWAGONS to roller coasters, Bob Stoops' first ride as a head coach has already been an interesting one.

Less than halfway through his first season at Oklahoma, Stoops has watched the number of bandwagon passengers fluctuate dramatically.

You couldn't find a seat after the Sooners started 3-0. But it's not as tough a ticket these days, after OU blew double-digit leads in losses to Notre Dame and Texas.

Stoops has a message for those no longer along for the ride: He warned that this could happen.

"I've said all along that we have to grow into everything we are doing," Stoops told Big 12 Conference media members on this week's teleconference. "What's frustrating is that we haven't had that many weeks in our system. But you hope to grow and get better as time goes on.

"Usually, the good teams do improve as the year goes on. And with us only being here a short while, I hoping that's the case ... that we will get better and make fewer mistakes the more familiar we get with everything that we are doing."

Stoops said he intends to spend the open date speaking to those riders he cares about most: his players.

"What our players have to be careful of is riding the roller coaster with the media and the fans," Stoops said. "The media for three weeks wanted to tell them how good they were, and that they were this and that and a Top 25 team.

"But I was saying the whole time that no, we've got to get better, we need to improve."

Stoops said he's been forced to take over at the wheel after the Sooners lost to teams he labeled as good. Notre Dame is 3-3, Texas 5-2.

"Now, all of a sudden, everyone wants to say that they (OU players) aren't any good," Stoops said. "So now I've got to argue with the media and tell them that they are good."

Stoops acknowledged that some of the criticism is deserved. That's why he doesn't want anyone apologizing for an OU defense that some have suggested has faltered the past two weeks because a sputtering OU offense forced it to stay on the field too long.

"I don't want to buy into that because I'm not going to make an excuse for our players and I don't want them having any excuses," he said. "I always put it back on them; it's their job to get off the field.

"To get (offenses) to go three-and-out or to get a turnover when we've got an opportunity to get one, that gets you off the field."

Stoops also isn't in the mood to make excuses for an offense that has seen its second-half production drop off against the Irish and the Longhorns. Improving an anemic running game, he said, will be an area of emphasis during the open week.

"Offensively, we've got to be more consistent in everything we do," Stoops said. "At times it looks great. And at times we allow people to get us in three-and-outs.

"Our offense is designed to eat up the clock and work the ball, and (to do that) we've got to get better running the football. So, hopefully, we can maintain more balance."

Stoops said he isn't too concerned that the players haven't maintained their emotional equilibrium in an uneven first half of the season.

"I think we're fine," he said. "Obviously, our confidence right now can't be great. But I don't think it's as bad as people want to say it is.

Fans should hang on tight. Stoops' background and competitive nature suggest this ride could get real interesting over the next seven weeks.

SLY STOOPS FAKES WAY TO SUCCESS

By Berry Tramel
The Daily Oklahoman, Oct. 27, 1999

NORMAN — Bob Stoops looks the part of football coach. Sharp dresser. Short hair. Decent tan.

He talks the part. Execution. Preparation. Talk a lot, don't say much.

He seems the part. Good squad. Getting better.

But Bob Stoops is a fraud. If ever he was a card-carrying member of the coaches association, it's been revoked. A coach? He's revealed himself to be no such thing.

Football coaches don't fake field goals. They don't fake punts. And if they do, they sure don't do it again.

A football coach faking a field goal is like asking for ketchup at a steak joint. Like going to the prom in an '84 Ford station wagon. Like admitting you watch Baywatch.

It just isn't done.

But Stoops keeps doing it. He fakes so many field goals, we're surprised when his Sooners do kick it. Stoops' idea of throwing us off is to fake a punt after he's faked a field goal.

Six games into his head coaching career, Stoops has ordered three fake field goals and one fake punt. He plays it as straight as a San Francisco street. As orthodox as a plaid wedding dress.

Stoops went to the Cotton Bowl 18 days ago and had his kicker catch a touchdown pass. Someone pass Barry Switzer the heart medication.

Switzer got to where he wouldn't throw to Tinker Owens or Keith Jackson in the Cotton Bowl, and Stoops is throwing to Tim Duncan with Bevo standing not 10 yards away?

And it wasn't Cotton Bowl fever. Last week against Texas A&M, Stoops faked a field goal and a punt. He's now 3-for-3 on fake field goals; 1-for-1 on fake punts.

Has anyone ever faked a field goal and a punt in the same game? Heck, yeah. Back in 1983, Illinois State came to Skelly Stadium and went home a 39-25 loser to Tulsa. But Redbird coach Bob Otolski gave it the old college try. He faked a field goal and a punt; both failed and soon Otolski went on to great things in the insurance business.

Stoops claims to be a by-the-book coach. Switzer's book was Jim Mackenzie's winning edge: a 20-item code. No. 1 on the list: Play the Percentages!

Switzer was a maverick in a lot of ways. He scrapped an offense in midseason and went to the wishbone. He recruited blacks and made them quarterbacks and captains when Texas and Arkansas would do nothing of the sort.

But on the field, Switzer was conservative. He punted when it was time to punt. He kicked a field goal when it was time to kick a field goal. He ran when it was time to run. He ran when it was time to pass.

Drive-by research has found no Sooner fake field goals between 1981 and Stoops, and memory serves none before then.

Stoops says the same things Switzer coached by, that a fake is fine "if you feel the percentages are pretty good." Does the potential benefit outweigh the potential loss?

"If it doesn't work, we lose momentum, we lose the game, then it's criticized," Stoops said.

Bob Simmons knows the criticism. His only bedlam loss came in 1996, when a fake field goal failed, Oklahoma State's momentum was zapped and the Sooners won, 27-17, in Stillwater. Simmons hasn't faked one since. "Make it, you're a hero," he said. "Don't make it, then (it's) why'd you do it?"

Kansas beat OSU, 13-6, in 1993, and the game's only touchdown was set up by a fake field goal. "It took some nerve," KU coach Glen Mason admitted, "and probably not much brains."

Colorado beat OSU, 16-12, in 1991 on a 20-yard touchdown pass off a fake field goal with 12 seconds left in the game. That's right; the Buffs trailed by two, and still Bill McCartney ordered a fake. A CU assistant said, "Only a man with a 15-year contract makes that call."

Shoot, what some folks consider the greatest team of all time, the '83 Nebraska Cornhuskers, needed a fake field goal to prolong their first touchdown drive against Oklahoma, en route to a 28-21 victory.

So fake field goals aren't extinct. But Stoops' are like strange rangers in New York City. It's not that you see one, it's that you see so many .

Three in the last five games. Two in consecutive showdowns against Texas and Texas A&M. All successful.

Which makes us ponder a point. Are we witnessing cultural change? Is Stoops way ahead of the game? Is he a pioneer?

I mean, everything from the forward pass to the facemask has been labeled a gimmick, but now they're more common than cleats and grass. Who said you can't fake a field goal every couple of quarters? Bob Stoops is proving otherwise.

Stoops, of course, claims no such thing. He still talks like a coach. He says you might see a fake field goal Saturday against Colorado, or you might never see another one. It all comes down to the percentages.

Maybe so. I prefer the pioneer theory. This Bob Stoops, he's a sly one.

OU

YOUNGSTOWN INSTILLED GUTS, GLORY IN STOOPSES

By Jenni Carlson
The Daily Oklahoman, Dec. 19, 1999

YOUNGSTOWN, OHIO — Around here, they are Ronnie and Bobby, Mike and Mark. They are Ron and Dee's boys. The kids from Detroit Avenue. The defensive backs from Cardinal Mooney.

They are the Stoops brothers.

We, of course, know two of the boys in quite a different light. Bob Stoops as the head coach at Oklahoma and Mike Stoops as his co-defensive coordinator. We know them as leaders of the Sooners' resurgence.

But the reasons for that can be found right here. Here, under skies that always seem to threaten rain, in the shadow of old steel mills, on the northeastern edge of Ohio, in the Stoopses' hometown.

Youngstown.

"This town is resilient," Ron Stoops Jr. said. "It's gone through a lot of hard times, but it's an extremely proud community. Keep working hard and things will work out for you. That's really what this area's about. That kind of precipitates through all the kids, not just our family. They all take that pride in Youngstown with them."

WORK ETHIC

Youngstown always has been a hard-working city.

Shortly after pioneers from the Western Reserve of Connecticut settled the area along the Mahoning River in 1797, they discovered pockets of iron ore. But it wasn't until they found great deposits of limestone that Youngstown had the raw materials necessary to become an iron and steel mecca.

The Stoopses' ancestors migrated to Youngstown, settling on the east side, becoming part of the blue-collar work force and instilling the town's values on their children.

Like his brothers, Ron Stoops Sr. took those values to heart. He went to East High School and didn't just become a good football player or a good baseball player. He became a multi-sport star. Football. Baseball. Basketball. He did it all.

And he did it all for a while in college. All three sports at Youngstown State University.

Baseball, however, became Ron Stoops' sport. He loved the others, but boy, could he play baseball. His cannon arm made him a standout shortstop. He even got a major league tryout.

But he didn't go. He couldn't. Not with his wife, Dee, in Youngstown.

She'd grown up on the east side, too, but had gone to a private school, a parochial school, Ursuline. That didn't matter to Ron, who was Catholic as well, and it surely didn't matter to Dee where Ron had gone to school.

They were in love.

"Faith and family were important," Dee said. "Everything else seemed to fall into place."

EAST SIDE KIDS

Ron and Dee wanted to raise their kids on the east side.

So they bought a house several miles south of their old neighborhoods. It was a Cape Cod, two bedrooms downstairs and a dormitory-style bedroom upstairs, a garage out back and a small, covered porch in the front.

It wasn't at all like most of the houses in Youngstown. It wasn't a towering two- or three-story giant.

No, it's so small, that house at 865 Detroit Avenue, that you have to wonder what would've happened if the Stoops boys had been linemen instead of defensive backs.

"Those guys were all sticks back then," said Jim Braydich, who lived two houses away, east toward Zedaker Street. "They're still skinny now, but those guys were sticks. They probably could have fit them all in one big double bed."

Braydich laughed.

"We weren't in the house much anyway."

That's no lie. The four Stoops boys and the five Braydich boys and several more in the neighborhood were forever playing kickball or football or basketball or whatever else they might want to do. They might play in the street or in someone's driveway. Even when the cold Ohio winters set in and the snow fell and the wind blew, it didn't stop them.

The boys would shovel Braydich's driveway, which had one of the neighborhood's few basketball goals. But it got so cold sometimes that the balls wouldn't bounce. They'd hit concrete with a hollow thud.

So they'd go down in the basement, turn the hot water on — full blast — and let it run over the basketball.

"We'd get outside," Braydich said, "and they'd be bouncin' to the sky. We'd get blisters on our fingers. Our fingers would crack.

"It was so cold."

The cold didn't stop them, and neither did the heat.

Down the street, past the Braydiches', was the park. Pemberton Park.

It might as well have been called Heaven. It had a pool and baseball fields and football fields and wide-open spaces and the woods. The woods were the place to be on most summer days. The kids would disappear down there for hours at a time.

Once, they discovered a mysterious plant. It was great. You could pull it out of the ground, and its root was sharp, sharp like a spear.

And so there they were, throwing these plants like javelins at each other. Which was all fine and dandy until Bobby took one in the head.

Lucky for him, Braydich's mother was a nurse. She butterflied his head and sent him on his way.

"It wasn't an easy neighborhood," said Renee Farragher, Bobby and Mike's younger sister. "You had to scrap for every bit of respect. There was always somebody older and tougher."

COMPETITION

As tough as the neighborhood was, it wasn't tough in today's vernacular.

"Not like some of these inner-cities," Ron Jr. said. "It definitely was a sports-oriented kind of tough. You had to survive. And you learned to compete."

It didn't matter if they were older or bigger or better. You still went after them. That came from living in the neighborhood and from living under Ron Stoops' roof.

"He was just so competitive," said Tony Congemi, a longtime assistant football coach at Cardinal Mooney High School. "We used to have a golf game — me, him, his brother and a neighbor. There were times where they were ready to go after each other.

"And that's how things were. That carried over to the boys."

Did it ever. Like Ron Jr. before them, Bobby and Mike went to Cardinal Mooney, the high school football powerhouse in Youngstown. The Cardinals had won city championships, Steel Valley titles and even one state title by the time Bobby and Mike started school there.

And instrumental to that success was Ron Sr. He became an assistant football coach in 1959 and took complete control of the defense when Don Bucci became the head coach in 1966.

"Ron," Bucci said, "that's yours."

Ron Sr. loved it. He had opportunities to become a head coach elsewhere but never went. You see, he had all the responsibility and benefit of being a head coach without all the headaches. No parents calling. No criticism flowing. No one noticing.He could just coach, tape ankles and clean lockers and wash towels and tell jokes and study film.

Oh, how he could study film.

"In the 1980's, when the computers were startin' to come in ... a couple people offered to buy us computers," said Bucci, who is still coaching at Mooney and now has four state titles and a .785 winning percentage. "Ron could start computerizing all the defensive sets, the tendencies.

"He didn't want any part of it. He wanted to do it — break down every film himself, jot down every play that a team would run — so he could get a feel for how he would call the defenses. He just had that feel."

A SPECIAL TEACHER

He was something special. A student. A teacher. A motivator.

Ron Stoops Sr. could make kids want to play so, so hard.

That expectation of excellence and respectable behavior was only magnified in his sons. Magnified in all of his children, really.

"We were never grounded," sister Renee said. "Just the look mom would give or my father would give was enough of a punishment. We just knew. It was expected.

"That's the driving force in all of us. It was never that we had to or that it was expected. We did it to make them happy. They sacrificed so much for us, I don't think any of us could've turned around and screwed up our lives."

And so, the Stoopses excelled.

For the boys, it was athletics. And they weren't exactly great athletes.

"They were not superstars," said Pete Mollica, long-time sports reporter at The Youngstown Vidicator. "They weren't the fastest kids. They weren't the biggest kids. But those were the type of kids that were 100 percent all of the time."

The Stoops boys made up for their shortcomings any way they could, any time they could.

Dee was packing the car one summer for the family's annual trip to the nearby shores of Lake Erie. With six growing children and all their stuff and the food, the car would be packed solid.

Then Bobby brought out his weights.

"What are those?" Dee asked, giving him one of her looks.

"Well," Bobby said, "they're goin' to the lake."

"Whaddaya mean they're goin' to the lake?" Dee said.

Despite her disagreement, those weights went to the lake.

"And they didn't just sit in the car or on the porch," Dee Stoops said. "He used those weights and ran the track every day. How 'bout that?

"He was driven."

Both Bobby and Mike were. And what they couldn't overcome physically, they compensated mentally.

"When you're that size," assistant coach Congemi said, "you have to be very intelligent. I think all ... of the boys understood their role on the defense, and the overall defense."

Congemi coached Mooney's defensive backs and can remember the boys talking about how easy the games were. The ease came from knowing exactly what teams were going to do. They knew the patterns, the blocks, the schemes.

"Everything was easy during the game," Congemi said, "because of the preparation, of what we did during the week. All they had to do was make the play."

MAKING THE PLAYS

And they made plenty of plays.

Fumble recoveries.

Interceptions.

Goal-line stands.

Bobby landed first-team Steel Valley honors as a senior in 1977, and Mike did the same two years later.

"It's a tossup between Mike and Mark," Bucci said of the two youngest brothers, "who was most talented.

"But Bobby was probably the toughest of them all. The hardest hitting. He loved for tight ends to come over the middle. He almost let 'em catch the ball and then pop 'em. He really enjoyed that. He probably was as good a safety as we've ever had here. And it was just based on the fact that he'd come up and he'd put you away."

Still, colleges weren't banging down Mooney's doors to sign Bobby Stoops. But Iowa and then-head coach Bob Commings took a chance on him. Commings, like Ron Sr. and Bucci, was an East High graduate, a Youngstown guy.

He knew what kind of players came out of Youngstown.

"This area's always been known for tough, good defensive football," Bucci said. "I doubt whether, for example, the football in Las Vegas is as hard-nosed or tough as it is here. High school football, it's an example of the area. It's tough."

And colleges knew that.

"They wouldn't come in here for backs and quarterbacks and all that," Bucci said. "They came to this area ... for the tough, tough, tough kid.

"That's where Bobby would fit in. Just a hard-nosed kid. And probably made it because he was."

Bob quickly became one of Iowa's defensive leaders, which brought the Hawkeyes back to Youngstown two years later when Mike graduated. Both went on to make All-Big Ten.

And even more importantly, the connections they made at Iowa helped them start coaching and helped them move to bigger and better programs and helped them land in Oklahoma.

"Oklahoma, wow," Dee Stoops said. "We used to watch all those big games, and Oklahoma was always in those big games.

"His dad would be so proud."

MEMORIES

Ron Sr. died in 1988.

Mooney was playing Boardman that September night. And it was quite a game. Ron Jr. just happened to be a coach at Boardman, where he still teaches and coaches. And so it was Stoops vs. Stoops, and it was intense and competitive and heartwrenching.

Maybe that's what got Ron Sr. Maybe his big, old heart just couldn't stand the thought of coaching against one of his own sons.

Maybe.

He had a heart attack and died on the football field.

Dee still lives in Youngstown.

Not in the old neighborhood but in a newer house. But reminders of days gone by, of times long passed, are everywhere. Pictures. Lots of pictures. Scrapbooks. And a poem.

Al Williamson, a Mooney grad and current faculty member, wrote it after Ron Sr.'s death.

> *All-American Father, that's what he is;*
> *A coach's coach, a man's man, a history whiz.*
> *A house painter, a friend-maker, a heck of a feller;*
> *Super salesman, serious worker, master joke teller ...*
> *But on a much larger scale his talents were needed.*
> *And if we reflect, we'll realize somehow:*
> *Old Ron's been promoted, and it only makes sense.*
> *God needs him now — to run His Defense.*

There's not a day, an hour, a moment that goes by that the Stoopses don't think about their father. Whether they are in still in Ohio like Ron Jr. and Renee and Kathy, or whether they are somewhere else, they are connected. They are tough. They are resilient.

Their father, their neighborhood, their Youngstown, taught them that.

"It isn't the tragedies in our lives," Dee Stoops said. "Everybody and every family is going to have those. It's how you handle them that's important."

Around here, that's the only way they want to be known.

STOOPS' SHOW IS A SOUND FOR SORE EARS

By Dave Sittler
The Daily Oklahoman, May 27, 1999

I F YOU are Bob Stoops and this is Thursday, it must be Enid. Or is it Idabel? How about Dallas, Guymon or Washington, D.C.?

Don't ask Stoops where he's been or where he's headed. Just point Oklahoma's new football coach in the direction of the next stop on the Sooners Caravan, the fund-raising, get-to-know-you tour that has Stoops making speeches across the state and nation.

"Who knows," Stoops said this week when asked how many stops he's made on a tour that doesn't end until late June. "I've quit counting. But it feels like I've been everywhere."

And everywhere Stoops has been, be it New York City or Ponca City, one part of his speech never changes:

"I'm not going to ask you to give me four or five years," Stoops tells fans and deep-pocket boosters. "I'm not that patient, and I know you aren't.

"I fully intend for us to be competitive and go after it next year. If that doesn't happen, I'll be as mad as you."

Stoops' speech must be a refreshing change for OU fans after what they endured on similar tours the last four years from Howard

Schnellenberger and John Blake.

Schnellenberger set the tone for his season of buffoonery at OU with outlandish statements. It was during the Tulsa stop Schnellenberger predicted that books would be written and movies made about his accomplishments in Norman.

Blake couldn't settle on offensive or defensive schemes, but his message never changed on the banquet circuit: "I love the kids on my team. Send me your kids, I'll take care of your kids. I love all my kids."

Stoops' talk falls someplace between Schnellenberger's far-out chats and Blake's love-in sessions. A place called reality. Down to earth, rational, believable.

Some might question the wisdom in Stoops' statement. They wonder why he doesn't plead for time to rebuild a once-proud program that Schnellenberger and Blake nearly reduced to rubble.

Even Schnellenberger and Blake said they needed time to recruit their players. Not Stoops. He continually repeats that OU intends to get it on from the first play of the season opener.

"You're right; it is different than what fans hear from some coaches," Stoops said. "Coaches like to pad themselves by saying, 'Hey, it will take of bunch of years to get my guys in here.' "

Stoops developed his get-after-it-now, no-excuses attitude while working for Steve Spurrier. Florida's coach has been called many things, but pessimistic and conservative are not among them.

"That's how Steve Spurrier is," Stoops said of Spurrier's supreme confidence. "He's right, and I believe in it."

Stoops acknowledged that the approach he adopted from Spurrier is directed as much at his team as the fans. And if media members want to cover his speeches, Stoops welcomes them to take down every word and report it.

"Players read newspapers; they know what's said," Stoops said. "If my players sit there for two or three months and read that I said, 'You (fans) need to give us four years before we'll win,' then it will take that long.

"Heck, my players don't want to hear that. More than anything, my seniors don't want to hear it. They want to come out and have a chance to win next season."

Winning in 1999 won't come easy for a couple of reasons: the lack of an abundance of quality talent and a difficult schedule. At least seven games figure to either be tossups or feature the Sooners as underdogs — Louisville, Notre Dame, Texas, Texas A&M, Colorado, Missouri and Oklahoma State.

Isn't Stoops, a rookie head coach, concerned his speech could come back to haunt him in late November?

"Are you kidding me?" he said. "It doesn't matter what I say; these people want to win next season and expect to win next season.

"If I stand there and tell people I don't expect to win, what kind of leader is that? That's just not my style."

From Norman to New York, is Stoops' optimistic style selling?

"Everyone is positive and enthusiastic," Stoops said. "But I don't know; all of this is new to me."

It isn't new to OU fans. It's just something they haven't heard in a long time.

STOOPS TACKLES INFLATED EXPECTATIONS

By George Schroeder
The Daily Oklahoman, July 13, 2000

Norman — He has been on the job for only 19 months, just one football season. But that's long enough to radically change fans' perceptions — and their expectations.

After a 7-5 season that included a trip to the Independence Bowl, Oklahoma coach Bob Stoops no longer is implored to make sure the Sooners put the right number of people on the field. Instead, they're asking if — no, when — OU will win another national championship.

No problem. Stoops is content with the direction of the program, convinced the Sooners are headed back to prominence. Personally, he's comfortable raising a young family in Norman, even as he maintains firm ties to his Ohio roots.

In a recent interview, Stoops discussed topics ranging from football to family — the two intertwined subjects in which he is most interested.

Q: Can you measure how fans' expectations have increased after last season's success?

A: I don't think there's any question. You hear and feel the pulse of everybody, from the media to the general public, that people are more upbeat and positive. Expectations now are rising. I like that. I've encouraged it. I've asked for it. I asked for it last year, for people to expect success, but I don't think anyone did. But now maybe they feel maybe he does know what he's talking about, and they should expect to win. So I welcome it and have no problem with it. The questions are different, remarks are different, everything's totally different. It's not even close.

Last year, there were people just wanting us to get 11 people on the field when we put a special team out there, and I felt we ought to be able to do more than that.

Q: Hearing those kinds of things must have struck you as unusual.

A: Yeah, it bothered me, because being a guy that grew up a long way from here in Ohio, I loved Oklahoma football. The reason all young kids like to watch a team is because they win, and they win championships. That's why I've always followed them, and then I got here and they just want me to get 11 guys out there on the field. They should expect more than that. We certainly did as a team and as coaches.

Q: You don't hear any of those requests any more?

A: No.

Q: Now you hear things like, "We want you to win a national championship?"

A: People are, I'm sure, still realistic. But they see we're headed in the right direction. And that's positive.

Q: Since you've been here, is there anything that's struck you about the history or tradition of OU football that you didn't already know before arriving in Norman?

A: I've enjoyed in one year reading and knowing more of Bud Wilkinson. Obviously, the age I am, I knew more of Barry Switzer than I did of Bud, though I certainly knew what he was and the great records he had. But I've been reading his book and hearing people talk of him and seeing what's around here on the walls. I have even more appreciation for what's been here before. The great teams, the great people, the person he was and a lot of the great people that played for him.

Q: You've been very active in getting some of those things placed on the walls, bringing in former players to speak, making sure the current players understand Sooner history. What's your reasoning behind that emphasis?

A: I think it's important for our players to know who they are. This is our tradition. Once you've been a member of this team, you're tied to all the other teams. I like the fact that they know they have this history and tradition to live up to, or at least to do their best to try to.

It's easy for some people to say "Well, that's in the past." It is, but it's our past. Just like you have family heritage and tradition in everyone's family that they try to live up to, well that's ours here. When you're a part of this team, you need to do your best to try to live up to those standards that have been set before you and create more. In the present, we need to create more. Hopefully, we can.

Q: Is it less difficult to bring OU back to prominence than to build a program where there isn't that tradition?

A: I think it always takes time and a lot of hard work and dedication and commitment from a lot of people — the president on down through the athletic director to the coaches and players. It takes a lot to rejuvenate anything. But I believe it can happen quicker when you do have tradition.

Q: College football's landscape has shifted since OU's decline. Do you hear from people who say the Sooners can't regain elite status?

A: I don't pay much attention to it. I don't know if anybody in America is going to win 47 straight games, I don't care what program they are. I think there's an understanding by most people that, yeah, things have changed from that standpoint.

But there's no reason we can't always be a factor in the Big 12 race. Then you have your years where you hit it just right and you're in the national championship. There's no reason that can't happen.

Q: Do you have anyone you consider a hero or mentor?

A: I don't know about hero. Some guys I consider mentors, guys I talk to an awful lot, would be Steve Spurrier, and Barry Alvarez is a very close friend and we talk on a number of issues. Another guy I was around when I was at Iowa and watched a lot was (Iowa wrestling coach) Dan Gable. I spent a lot of time in the wrestling room and around him.

Q: As a football coach, what do you take from a wrestling coach?

A: A lot. Just his intensity, the way he relates to players and motivates players. His thoughts of planning out his practices, how physical or how demanding from one time leading up to competition.

Q: Have you been involved with the OU wrestling program?

A: I know Jack Spates well and think an awful lot of him. I haven't been over there as much as I'd like. I haven't had the time, I guess. I had a lot more time when I was a graduate assistant and volunteer coach when I was at Iowa to watch Dan Gable.

Q: You come from a coaching family. Growing up, was it a foregone conclusion you would be a coach?

A: If I had a hero, it would be my father (Ron Stoops, who coached high school football for 30 years before his death in 1988). Growing up, it was easy to follow him or be around him. If I'm more like anybody, it's probably like him. I just sort of naturally gravitated toward this.

Q: Did you ever consider doing anything else?

A: Like a good number of college kids, my first couple of years I didn't know what I was going to do. I ended up with a business degree in marketing. But when it came time to graduate, I couldn't see myself in a normal job. I just felt I would miss the excitement, challenge and competition of sports. I know there's competition in business, but you don't get the finality of it week in and week out to see how you did. And I always enjoyed the strategies of football, the game-planning, the schemes of the game.

Q: You have a daughter (Mackenzie) who will turn 4 later this month and twin boys (Isaac and Drake) who turned 1 last month. Has that changed your perspective on family life or coaching football?

A: No, I've always felt I've been pretty balanced on family and work and all the obligations you have. I guess I'm just lucky to have three healthy children and a great marriage.

Q: Do you have any ideas about what your boys might end up doing?

A: No. I have no idea. Or my daughter, for that matter. Whatever they want. But around me, they'll be around ball. And when we're at my house, the driveway, we're shooting basketball. It's hard to play football all the time. Whatever they decide to do, that will be fine. I'm sure they'll find their way.

Q: How are you adjusting to Norman? How does it compare to some of the places you've lived?

A: It's a great town, a great college atmosphere. A wonderful city, and the people are just great. It offers a lot. You look at Oklahoma City being so close. It's nice to be able to go up to ball games. There are a lot of good restaurants in Norman and Oklahoma City, a lot of opportunities there. And then, the university has a lot to offer. So it's a great time.

Q: This time of year, you get a little more free time. When you're in town, how do you try to spend it?

A: Try and spend a little more time with my children and my wife. Take the kids to the zoo for a day or something.

Q: What's your idea of a perfect day of relaxation? If you had one?

A: The perfect day for me to relax would be golf at 8:30, a jog after golf — you've got to have a jog every day — and afterward to be with my wife, children and friends on my back porch for the rest of the afternoon.

Q: Do you get to have those kinds of days?

A: Not very often. I seem to get one or the other, but not all of it together. But it happens sometimes.

OU

STOOPS SWEARS BY THE SYSTEM, NOT THE COACH

By John Rohde
The Daily Oklahoman, Aug. 17, 2000

NORMAN — Oklahoma football coach Bob Stoops is extremely systematic.

He believes in having a system. He preaches it, pushes it, practices it. Most important, he believes in it.

This is why Stoops is rather appalled at the notion OU's offense will suffer with the departure of offensive coordinator Mike Leach.

"This is Oklahoma's offense, not Mike Leach's," Stoops has said. "It's been built around a system.

"When I was (defensive coordinator) at Florida, some people said it was my defense. It wasn't my defense. It was Florida's defense. I left, and it stayed."

Leach left to coach Texas Tech, and Stoops insists the OU offense stayed.

Mark Mangino now calls the shots as offensive coordinator.

Yes, the Sooners will run more often this season, or at least try. They would be trying to do the same thing if Leach were still in Norman.

All pass and no run is asking for trouble. Plus, why waste the talent of feature back Quentin Griffin?

In the evolution of football, which came first: The system or the player?

The answer is both. You can't have one without the other.

Logically, the system should come first.

Most college coaches implement a system, then recruit accordingly. Others gobble up as much talent as they can, then figure it out from there. Some coaches never figure it out.

Throughout much of the 1990's, Oklahoma struggled to figure it out. A carousel of coaches led to a carousel of quarterbacks.

Trivia: Who led OU in passing two years ago?

Wrong, it was Jake Sills.

For 10 seasons (1989-98), the Sooners offered a variety-pack behind center: Steve Collins, Tink Collins, Chris Melson, Cale Gundy, Garrick McGee, Terence Brown, Justin Fuente, Eric Moore, Brandon Daniels, Jarrod Reese, Patrick Fletcher, Sills, et al.

Imagine the instability had Gundy not been in the mix.

Stability has returned in Josh Heupel, born and raised in South Dakota and snatched from a po-dunk junior college in Utah.

Tragically, the Sooners have Heupel for only one more season.

Why was OU so successful offensively last year? Was it the system or Heupel?

Again, the answer is both.

"Josh Heupel really makes the system work efficiently," Mangino said. "He's just so dedicated to this. He's a self-starter.

"The system plays a part of it, but the success we've had in the past, a lot of it has to do with Josh Heupel."

Translation: No one could simply step in and post Heupel's outrageous numbers.

Georgia transfer Nate Hybl figures to be Heupel's heir apparent, with freshmen Jason White and Hunter Wall out to prove differently.

Will these replacements enjoy the same success as Heupel, or better?

Possibly.

We might get a sneak peek during OU's soft September schedule. That's when we'll see if it's the system, or Heupel, or both.

TWO STOOPSES ON SIDELINE ARE BETTER THAN ONE

By George Schroeder
The Daily Oklahoman, Aug. 27, 2000

NORMAN — When Bob Stoops became head coach at Oklahoma, he wasted no time asking his brother Mike to join him.

He had no choice. It was a mother's command.

"I told Bob, 'You're not taking a head job without Mike,' " Dee Stoops remembered.

Bob Stoops didn't need the prodding. The brothers had been together at Iowa and Kansas State. And before that, at home in Youngstown, Ohio.

This was simply the next step in a progression. Bob Stoops wanted to hire his brother. Mike Stoops wanted to work for his brother.

"They dreamed about it, and it happened," Dee Stoops said.

So far, OU's "Right Brothers" couldn't be happier about the arrangement.

"It's been easy," Bob Stoops said. "It's great. We're able to be around each other and share time."

Look at it this way: It's the family business, just like some brothers and sons grow up and run the family hardware store.

Only in the Stoops family, the family business is football.

Ron Stoops Sr. was a high school football coach for 30 years before his death in 1988. His four sons are now football coaches. Ron Jr. is an assistant coach at Boardman (Ohio) High School. Mark, the youngest, is defensive coordinator at Houston.

"We thought they would coach, and coach together," Dee Stoops said. "With six kids less than 10 years apart, you learn to share. We shared everything."

The arrangement isn't for everyone.

"I couldn't work with my brothers," OU co-defensive coordinator Brent Venables said, "and I love them dearly."

But if brothers can work together — and these guys obviously can — The benefits are obvious. Venables said head coaches pick assistants as much for "trust and loyalty as X's and O's.

"You want to know what you're getting," Venables said. "When you pull that trigger and make that decision, you have to hit a home-run ball."

That made hiring Mike an easy decision for Bob Stoops. He knows his brother better than anyone.

But that leads to this question: Do Bob and Mike Stoops interact as coaches, or brothers? Where and how do they draw a line?

"Sometimes it's just like another coach," Bob Stoops said. "Sometimes we have to watch it. We may get to talking about something and maybe end up arguing to each other like brothers, as opposed to a head coach and assistant coach. We'll always be brothers first."

Mike Stoops agreed.

"The brother in us comes out at times," he said. "We have arguments and disagreements, but we quickly resolve them like anybody. There are certain guidelines that you follow. I don't overstep those. I think we both have a mutual respect for one another's ideas."

Other members of OU's coaching staff say there aren't many arguments, no visible sibling rivalry. The brothers tend to think alike, both from their upbringing and from their similar football paths.

"They're on the same page almost all the time," Venables said.

Venables, who played for the Stoops brothers at Kansas State and then began coaching with them, has seen the Stoops brothers work together for almost a decade. And now that Bob Stoops is head coach, Venables said "nothing has changed at all."

He said Bob Stoops allows Mike Stoops and Venables defensive autonomy — with occasional input. But it's the same system they've been running for years, since Bob Stoops was Kansas State's defensive coordinator, Mike was an assistant and Venables was a defensive back.

"We've kind of followed the same circles, the same path," Mike Stoops said. "I still feel like I went out and did my own thing at K-State, had my own success. But I've studied a lot of what he does. We do a lot of similar things. That's where I got a lot of my ideas."

One day, Mike Stoops believes, he'll leave his brother and become a head coach. When that happens, Mark Stoops might become a hot coaching commodity.

"I'd imagine Bob would probably go after him first," Mike Stoops said. "We might have to battle. Mark might be in a good position there."

Wonder what Mom will say then?

DON'T EXPECT TOO MUCH OF STOOPS YET

By Berry Tramel
The Daily Oklahoman, Aug. 29, 2000

B OB STOOPS discovered oil. He taught Will Rogers to use a rope. And he ghost wrote "Oklahoma!" for Rodgers and Hammerstein.

How else to explain the runaway enthusiasm unleashed by Oklahoma fans over their second-year football coach. After a season in which his Sooners matched the 1999 record of Oregon State, Stoops has been elevated to Wilkinson/Switzer status.

The nation's best coach. The messiah. An unquestioned genius.

One question: How do we know that Stoops doesn't merely look good in a dim light? Not to be guilty of piling on, but who wouldn't look good following John Blake?

A beat-up jalopy rides pretty good when your sports car throws a rod or blows a gasket. Pork rinds taste divine when your beef-steak is burnt black.

Stoops took Blake's beat-down players, added a quarterback and put OU back in the bowl business. Lots of coaches could have done it; Stoops did do it, so give him credit. But put him in the College Football Hall of Fame?

Seems a bit premature.

Doesn't Stoops still have something to prove?

"Not in my mind," OU director of football operations Merv Johnson said Saturday. "Nothing has changed as far as the impressions I've had, really from Day One.

"The way he's been able to make players feel about themselves and their team, the confidence he's instilled."

Stoops' status soars beyond our state lines. In Iowa, for instance.

In December 1998, when OU and Iowa both sought a coach, the Sooners won the Stoops Derby, though he was a Hawkeye grad and adopted son. The Sooner coup caused much wailing and gnashing of teeth in corn country.

"Mass disappointment," said Chuck Long, who then was Iowa's quarterback coach and now is OU's. "Very simply, Oklahoma's gain and Iowa's loss.

"He is regarded elsewhere as a top coach in the country."

Stoops himself claims no need to prove himself and points not to 1999 for the evidence.

"I didn't feel I had to prove myself last year," Stoops said. "I felt comfortable with the experience of the people I've been around. I've been very fortunate with the quality of people I've been with. All have a history of success."

True enough. Stoops' mentors are as stout as anyone's could be. Hayden Fry at Iowa. Bill Snyder at Kansas State. Steve Spurrier at Florida. All took programs in various degrees of desolation to various degrees of national prominence.

And Stoops seems on the same road with the Sooners. In 20 months, he's changed the mindset. That's what Snyder has said was the big hurdle at K-State. Making 21-year-olds believe after they'd quit believing.

"The squad he inherited not only didn't feel good about themselves, but were embarrassed," Johnson said. "A deal you kind of wanted to hide your head."

Hidden heads now are held high. Yet it's early in the journey. Stoops might very well be the third-generation Sooner savior.

But a quiet cry rings through the praise. Call it not doubt but caution. Show us more.

DR. STOOPS GIVES SOONERS SHOT OF BELIEF

By Berry Tramel
The Daily Oklahoman, Oct. 18, 2000

H ER MAJESTY'S soldiers lay wounded in various degrees of injury as their colonel strolled through the 4077th M*A*S*H. He showed little compassion.

Up, chaps, he commanded. You're not hurt. Put this behind you and report back to the front.

Hawkeye Pierce was aghast. He upbraided the British officer's bedside manner. Have you no shame? No pity? No concern for your men?

Soon thereafter, Hawkeye entered the hospital to find the colonel sitting cotside, chatting and laughing with his lads, who were much improved.

What gives, Hawkeye asked. Simple, said the Brit. Treat the troops like they're healthy, and they will be. Expect them to rise and rise they will. Mind over matter. Positive attitude. You've got to believe.

British colonel, sir; meet your match. Dr. Bob Stoops has a Ph.D. in mental toughness. The Oklahoma football coach dispenses confidence to the firm and infirm.

Stoops treats his troops like quality ballplayers, thus they believe they are quality ballplayers. Expect them to succeed and success follows.

"Coach Stoops is a great teacher in psychology," said OU co-defensive coordinator Brent Venables. Venables played for and coached with Stoops at Kansas State, and now coaches with him at OU.

Thus Venables knows Stoops well. Public and private. Always, Venables said, Stoops "portrays great toughness, great confidence. Our kids have bought into it. He's planted the seeds enough, they recognize they're not so bad."

We live in a time of level playing fields. Parity reigns.

Minnesota leads the Big 10, South Carolina leads the SEC and TCU is the best team in Texas. Self-esteem isn't a supplement, it's college football's life blood. It's the difference between winning and losing.

Twenty-two months ago, Stoops took over a beaten-down band of Sooners and refused to acknowledge their wounds. Get up, let's go, victory awaits, he told them.

Now Oklahoma is 6-0 and ranked third nationally. Does OU have Top 3 talent? Who knows? Who cares? Talent is as talent does.

And OU's talent has thrashed Texas, 63-14, and Kansas State, 41-31, the last two Saturdays. The swagger is back.

Two years ago, the Sooners' confidence was shot. The final days of the John Blake era were plagued by scarred psyches.

Now many of the same players are ready for all comers.

"That was a gradual process," said safety Roy Williams. "At first, some guys missed coach Blake. But once we got under coach Stoops' wing, everybody started believing in the system."

Hope was the theme of the Blake years. Things will get better, Blake said. Suffer now, but the payoff will come.

Bullfeathers, Stoops says. Hope sinks. Hope to him is a four-letter word.

"We didn't come up here hoping," Stoops said Saturday in Manhattan, Kan.

Stoops has swiped a theme traditionally reserved for fans. Win now. Forget patience. Get up off your sickbed, lads. We've got a war to win.

SOONERS' FOOTBALL SUCCESS LEADS TO REWARD FOR COACH

By Steve Lackmeyer
The Daily Oklahoman, Nov. 1, 2000

TULSA — Sooner fans aren't the only ones who love Bob Stoops.

The coach who turned around a fading football team and restored it to national prominence is now also one of the country's highest-paid college coaches — and a millionaire.

The University of Oklahoma Board of Regents doubled Stoops' guaranteed annual salary Tuesday, from $675,000 to $1.4 million.

OU President David Boren said the new five-year contract extension was already in the works before Stoops led the Sooners to victories over the nation's 10th-, second- and top-rated teams, landing the team at No. 1 in the country this week.

"We ought to express our appreciation," Boren said after regents unanimously approved the pay hike at their meeting in Schusterman Center in Tulsa. "If we know we are going to do this if someone came after him and we offer it as a counteroffer, why not go ahead and pay him what he is worth?"

Boren said Stoops' contributions go beyond regaining the Sooners' past glory, saying the coach has restored the athletic department's self-sufficiency and boosted OU's pride and image.

"The main thing, more than anything else, he is the right person for our university," Boren said. "When you look out a decade ahead, he is the person we want to symbolize the University of Oklahoma."

The pay hike will be funded by the university's athletic department, which struggled with deficits for a decade before Stoops' arrival.

The new contract, which runs through Dec. 31, 2005, calls for Stoops' state salary to remain at $200,000. The remainder of the guaranteed salary goes up from $475,000 to $1.2 million. The potential amount of performance-based bonuses, meanwhile, goes up from $250,000 to in excess of $300,000.

Such bonuses would be based on winning "Coach of the Year," team academics and championships. And, to sweeten the pot even more, the deal also pays Stoops a one-time $200,000 bonus upon execution of the contract, which has been signed by Stoops.

"I appreciate and I'm very confident about the leadership of this university," Stoops said. "And I'm grateful to be here, because it's a great football job."

Both Boren and OU Athletic Director Joe Castiglione estimated the new salary places Stoops among the nation's five highest-paid college coaches. To be exact, it ranks him third behind Steve Spurrier of the University of Florida, $2.1 million, and Bobby Bowden of Florida State, $1.5 million.

Castiglione joked that the new salary was established using "a big pencil."

"This whole approach has been very thoughtful and mindful of the marketplace and market forces," Castiglione said.

"We evaluated our situation against the nation's best competition, and that's the realm in which we consider ourselves in trying to be at the top,"

"Football, unlike any other sport we sponsor, because of sheer numbers, the tradition of success, contributions tied directly or indirectly to the football program's success, visibility, interest and exposure, all relate to increases in revenue (for the university)."

Castiglione said Stoops' new salary should be evaluated in terms of the team's current fortune, as well as its failures throughout the past decade.

"There had been a price for failure. And there is a price for success," Castiglione said. "I'll leave it up to the eye of the beholder as to which one they value most."

STOOPS NAMED BIG 12 COACH OF THE YEAR

By Owen Canfield
The Associated Press, Nov. 30, 2000

NORMAN — BOB Stoops needed just one season to make the Oklahoma Sooners respectable in the Big 12. In his second season, the Sooners are more than respectable — they're ranked No. 1 in the country, and Stoops is the overwhelming choice as AP's Big 12 coach of the year.

Stoops received 17 of 20 votes in balloting by sportswriters throughout the conference region. Dan McCarney, who led Iowa State to an 8-3 season and its first bowl game since 1978, received the other three votes.

"That's an award that to me is given to the entire coaching staff," Stoops said. "I'm appreciative and honored. I'm fortunate to work with the guys I work with every day. These coaches are excellent. We've got a great rapport in our office and our day-to-day working environment."

When Stoops took over as OU's coach in December 1998, he inherited a program that had won just 12 games in the previous three years

"There are three factors that I think have made him successful here," offensive coordinator Mark Mangino said. "The first one is his positive attitude. The second thing is that he doesn't accept excuses for anything. If you fail at something or don't get it done, then you didn't get it done.

"The third thing is he came in here and embraced the tradition and high expectations of OU. He didn't come in and say 'We're going to have to wait a while until we recruit our own players.' "

STOOPS, HEUPEL WIN WALTER CAMP AWARDS

By George Schroeder
The Daily Oklahoman, Nov. 28, 2000

NORMAN — The awards are beginning to roll in.

Today, Oklahoma senior quarterback Josh Heupel was named the Walter Camp Foundation's national player of the year. The award was presented during the Sooners' weekly press luncheon.

OU coach Bob Stoops was named the organization's national coach of the year. It's only the third time in 34 years a player and coach from the same school have been honored.

They'll be formally honored at the 34th national awards banquet Feb. 10 on the Yale University campus in New Haven, Conn.

Bernard Pellegrino, the Walter Camp Foundation's president, presented Heupel with the trophy. He said the quarterback was the "overwhelming" choice in a vote of NCAA Division I-A coaches and sports information directors.

It was the first of two national honors for Heupel on Tuesday. He also was named The Sporting News' player of the year.

Heupel becomes the third OU player named the Walter Camp player of the year, joining Steve Owens in 1969 and Billy Sims in 1978.

Both of those players went on to win the Heisman Trophy, an

award for which Heupel is considered a leading candidate. But they're not the only Heisman connection. The last nine Walter Camp winners won the Heisman.

When presented with the trophy, Heupel quickly deflected praise to God, teammates and coaches.

"Individual awards are indicative of what's gone on in your entire football program," Heupel said. "It's a tremendous honor to this football team to compliment them in such a manner for what they've done in the past year statistically. I'd also like to thank my lord and savior Jesus Christ for showering me with blessings on this earth, especially the past two years."

It was left to Stoops and Heupel's teammates to praise Heupel, who leads the NCAA with a 65.8-percent completion rate, ranks fifth in total offense (300.6 yards per game) and total passing (23.7 completions per game), third in yards per attempt (8.9) and 13th in passing efficiency.

Stoops said Heupel should receive much of the credit for OU's rise to the top of the rankings less than two years after three consecutive losing seasons.

Said Stoops: "For Josh to receive this award is extremely special. It tells you what a guy like Josh has done for our program. He won't sit up there and talk about it, but I feel compelled to. You look at where this program has come in two years, and there are a lot of reasons.

"But our success this season and for us to be in position we're in, the only team in the country that's undefeated ... to play the tremendous schedule we've had and to emerge unscathed through it all, Josh Heupel is the main reason for that."

STOOPS IS NATIONAL COACH OF THE YEAR

By Jenni Carlson
The Daily Oklahoman, Dec. 8, 2000

LAKE BUENA VISTA, Fla. — Bob Stoops has always taken after his father where coaching is concerned.

The Oklahoma coach did something Thursday at the Home Depot College Football Awards Show that Ron Stoops never did. Stoops won an award for coach of the year.

Ron Sr. was a longtime defensive coordinator for Cardinal Mooney High School in Youngstown, Ohio.

"They don't give a lot of awards for that," Stoops said.

But they give plenty of awards for what Stoops has done. In only his second year at OU, Stoops has led the Sooners from a string of three losing seasons to a chance at a national championship. The Sooners are undefeated, top-ranked and headed to the Orange Bowl.

Stoops won the George Munger Award for college coach of the year, which is presented by the Robert W. Maxwell Football Club. He received 623 of the 864 votes, a whopping 72 percent.

Miami (Fla.) coach Butch Davis was second with 64 votes.

"This isn't just to me," Stoops said. "I don't look at it that way. It means more to the team and the assistant coaches."

STOOPS ADDS AP COACH AWARD TO TROPHY CASE

By Richard Rosenblatt
The Associated Press, Dec. 12, 2000

N EW YORK — Bob Stoops didn't need long to prove he could turn awful into awesome at Oklahoma.

In just his second season as a head coach, Stoops guided the Sooners (12-0) to the No. 1 ranking, a perfect regular season and a shot at their first national championship since 1985 when they play Florida State in the Orange Bowl on Jan. 3.

"I feel a sense of pride for the way these players have worked," Stoops said, "and for the guys who have been around for a few years who were told they weren't very good. We are now a confident bunch."

Today, the 40-year-old Stoops was chosen Associated Press college coach of the year in balloting by AP member newspapers, TV and radio stations.

Stoops, who brought a wide-open passing attack to a school known for its wishbone and option running game, received 41 of the 91 votes in the AP balloting.

South Carolina's Lou Holtz was second with 19 votes, and Oregon State's Dennis Erickson was third with 16 votes.

"It's a great honor for Oklahoma," Stoops said. "It's an award that every assistant coach has a piece of, and it reflects on the players and their attitude about working together, about the way they won. The trophy will go in the coaches' hallway, not in my house."

Last week, Oklahoma quarterback Josh Heupel was selected the AP's college player of the year.

Stoops, a highly regarded defensive coordinator under Kansas State's Bill Snyder and then Florida's Steve Spurrier, accepted the challenge of returning Oklahoma to its winning ways. A school with six national titles had fallen on hard times under John Blake, losing 22 of 34 games from 1996-98.

On the day he took over, Dec. 1, 1998, Stoops said "there should be great expectations here. It's a program with the championships that should expect championships. I know we'll operate with no excuses. There are no excuses. You succeed or you don't."

Success arrived quickly. In 1999, Stoops unveiled his passing game directed by Heupel, a star at Snow Junior College in Utah but unknown just about everywhere else. The Sooners went 7-5, Heupel broke a bunch of school passing records and OU played in its first bowl game since 1994.

This season, Stoops said his players were better prepared and more disciplined. Even with a three-game run against Big 12 Conference powers Texas, Kansas State and Nebraska, Stoops knew his team would not be intimidated.

"People were looking at a piece of paper saying 'they can win this one, they can't win that one,'" Stoops said. "We see our kids every day. They pushed themselves hard in the off-season and earned the right to be confident. Last year, we were not good enough to hold leads, we were not disciplined enough to finish off games. We knew we would be better."

No. 19 in the preseason poll, the Sooners moved up to No. 10 with easy wins over Texas-El Paso, Arkansas State, Rice and Kansas. Next up, a No. 11 Texas, followed by a No. 2 Kansas State, then a showdown against No. 1 Nebraska.

No problem. The Sooner magic of the 1970's and '80 returned. OU toppled the Longhorns, 63-14, in Dallas; won at Kansas State,

41-31; returned home to dominate the Cornhuskers, 31-14; and took over the No. 1 ranking.

In those games, Heupel threw for 949 yards, four TD's and just one interception as he became a top Heisman Trophy contender. He finished second to Florida State's Chris Weinke.

Before the Nebraska game, Stoops showed his team films of the classic OU-NU games from the 1970's and 1980's. "The kids didn't really know what it was all about," Stoops said. "We wanted them to know."

The Sooners had a shaky finish — a comeback 35-31 win at Texas A&M followed by closer-than-expected calls against Texas Tech and Oklahoma State. Then it was on to the Big 12 title game, with K-State waiting for revenge. Heupel overcame three interceptions with two TD's passing and one rushing for a 27-24 win and a berth in the BCS' title game in Miami.

Stoops says the win over Texas may have been the turning point.

"As much as anything else, I remember them not being in awe against Texas," Stoops said. "We told them, 'You are one of the elite teams. You are Oklahoma.' We have won a lot of big games at Oklahoma. We fully expected to win, and the way we did we knew the next two games that we ought to be able to get 'em."

STOOPS EARNS BONUS FOR CHAMPION SEASON

By George Schroeder
The Daily Oklahoman, Dec. 17, 2000

N ORMAN — Oklahoma coach Bob Stoops said he would give plenty for a national championship.

"If I could win it, I'd gladly give up 'X' amount of dollars," Stoops said.

If OU beats Florida State in the Orange Bowl Jan. 3, Stoops will receive plenty.

An incentive clause in Stoops' recently renegotiated contract promises the coach $150,000 if the Sooners win the national championship. He's already guaranteed $100,000 for OU's participation in the title game.

Those are some of the performance bonuses that could allow Stoops to earn as much as $1.957 million this year. Stoops' contract, approved by the OU Board of Regents on Oct. 31, guarantees $1.4 million annually for five years plus a generous batch of incentives.

Stoops is almost certain to gain $50,000 for a top-10 finish in the BCS' final national rankings.

Stoops said he is "not very much aware" of the incentives — "I don't pay any attention to them, to be honest," he said — and said he plans to share some of the rewards with his assistant coaches.

It's all part of a contract that athletic director Joe Castiglione said reflects the school's appreciation for Stoops' accomplishments.

"He's a complete package, and we recognize that," Castiglione said of Stoops. "That's why we've provided what we believe to be the complete package."

Castiglione doesn't begrudge Stoops' extra compensation. It's likely OU will more than make up for the incentives.

"The university understands the increases in future revenue will have some tieback to extraordinary accomplishments," Castiglione said. "Therefore, we make decisions to include monetary incentives for different levels of performance. I don't think anyone would argue with an employer rewarding one of its leaders in taking their team to the top."

Castiglione said Stoops' contract ranks third nationally, behind Florida's Steve Spurrier ($2.1 million) and Florida State's Bobby Bowden ($1.5 million) — although Castiglione said he hasn't evaluated Texas coach Mack Brown's recent raise to a reported $1.45 million.

Stoops' deal features a $200,000 base salary, an increase of $25,000 from the previous deal.

He is also guaranteed $600,000 for personal services including radio/television/Internet programs and endorsement appearances; speaking engagements; and shoe, equipment and apparel consulting agreements. That's an increase of $250,000. The contract stipulates Stoops must report all athletic-related income from outside sources (which will be included in the $600,000 total).

Stoops is guaranteed an additional $600,000 for appearances and speaking engagements on behalf of OU unrelated to athletics, an increase of $500,000. Stoops can also receive additional compensation from summer football camps.

Stoops also received a $200,000 signing bonus.

The contract also provides: two automobiles and insurance for use by Stoops and his wife, Carol Stoops; membership and monthly dues at an area golf course; and 20 football tickets.

Another potential performance bonus: $10,000 for a graduation rate of 70 percent or better. That will be based on NCAA figures and won't be applicable for several years.

If OU fires Stoops, it must pay $1.5 million.

But one thing the five-year contract doesn't include is a large buy-out clause if Stoops leaves. When Alabama hired TCU's Dennis Franchione last month, the Crimson Tide paid TCU $1 million.

By comparison, Stoops' contract requires a buyout equal to one year's base salary: $200,000; if he were to leave before Dec. 1, 2001, he would also have to repay the $200,000 signing bonus.

OU assistants' salaries, which rank third in the Big 12 and compare favorably with top schools in other major conferences, will be increased after the season. And in October, the school announced a $100 million athletic facilities project that includes about $50 million for expansion and renovation to Memorial Stadium and other football-related projects.

"We always know that there are other possibilities," Castiglione said. "We're very aware of the market forces. More importantly, we're focused on what we want for this program .... It's not about direct financial compensation for a coach. It's the rest of the commitment. It's about making this environment so good that no one would really ever want to leave. We believe we're creating an atmosphere that is so good that few would ever consider leaving."

SOONERS' COACH IS A LEGEND IN THE MAKING

By George Schroeder
The Daily Oklahoman, Jan. 2, 2001

M IAMI — Not so long ago, someone came to Bob Stoops with a proposition. He wanted to put Stoops' likeness on a poster along with those of Bud Wilkinson and Barry Switzer.

Stoops agreed, albeit uncomfortably, when he learned the proceeds would go to charity. But he wasn't ready to accept the poster's premise: that Stoops, midway through his second season as Oklahoma's coach — in his second season as a head coach, period — had achieved equal status with the Sooners' coaching legends.

"I don't feel I deserve to be linked with them," Stoops said. "Those guys stood for winning championships for a number of years.

I don't think I've earned that. Those guys have earned that, and I've got a long way to go before I do."

That's true. Wilkinson and Switzer each coached the Sooners to three national championships. But Stoops has the Sooners on the verge of the school's seventh title.

Wednesday evening, top-ranked OU plays No. 3 Florida State in the Orange Bowl, with the Bowl Championship Series' national championship at stake. After a decade of decline, the Sooners are again among college football's elite.

It's no wonder that back home in Oklahoma, Stoops has quickly risen to exalted status. "Stoops for President" signs have become common. That poster? Stoops thought it would be a limited publication, something for a class project. Instead, he's seen it in many places, a hot seller.

But what about outside of our patch of the heartland? We know how much of the nation looks upon Switzer. What do they think of Stoops?

He's a rising star. Witness the number of coach of the year awards Stoops has won or is in contention to win.

"He's got a national reputation now," said Grant Teaff, the former Baylor coach who is executive director of the American Football Coaches Association.

College football insiders say they have long known of Stoops, that he built a reputation with his defensive achievements as coordinator at Kansas State and Florida.

"He might be a new household name, but he's been a part of successful programs for a number of years," OU athletic director Joe Castiglione said. "People who follow college football are very much aware of Bob's coaching prowess."

But that's different, Teaff said, from making a name as a head coach.

"He was a person people in the know would say has got a chance," Teaff said. "Not everybody's a head coach. Just to shine as a bright star as an assistant coach doesn't mean you're a head coach.

"The last two years mean he's a head coach."

Stoops probably burst upon the nation's consciousness at about the same time his team did: in October.

First, the eyes of Texas were drawn to Stoops. A week later, the Sooners popped Kansas State and Stoops' longtime boss, Bill Snyder. Two weeks later, with a 31-14 defeat of No. 1 Nebraska and the Sooners' subsequent vault to the top ranking they still hold, Stoops was suddenly a hot commodity.

Here's one telling example: Dean Blevins, the former Sooner

quarterback and News9 and CBS college football analyst, recalls a conversation he had in the summer of 1999 with ABC television commentator Brent Musburger.

Musburger asked Blevins what he thought about Stoops and how good he thought OU would be. Blevins said he believed Stoops would bring the Sooners back to prominence.

"Brent laughed at me," Blevins recalled.

Blevins had the last laugh.

"Midway through this season, Brent called me," Blevins said. "He said, 'You were right. The guy can coach.' "

While Stoops, 40, is considered a hot young coach — the hot young coach — that status comes without the location that usually accompanies the tag. Stoops isn't at a stepping-stone school, doesn't appear to be looking toward the next upward move.

He has embraced OU's tradition and appears set on restoring it and adding a new chapter to it.

Many people believe Stoops will succeed. Florida State coach Bobby Bowden is among them.

Now, Stoops is matched against Bowden, a coaching legend. Bowden has built Florida State from nothing to national titles. He appears on track to one day become college football's all-time winningest coach.

Bowden said Stoops' coaching performance reminds him of how he started at Florida State, only Stoops' progress has come more quickly.

But Bowden believes he has identified what might be the most important factor in Stoops' success.

"It's very obvious. He's so positive," Bowden said. "He doesn't give you a drop of a negative feeling. Twelve-point favorite? That don't bother him. He's been through that five times already this year.

"He's changed the minds of his players. That's the starting place."

That optimism comes from confidence — "I'm not a worrier," Stoops said — that might be what allowed him to embrace OU's tradition without any insecurity.

There's a photograph hanging on a wall in Stoops' home. Taken the day he accepted the OU job, it shows Stoops making remarks to Sooner fans. Behind him, looking over his shoulder, is Switzer.

"I still look at it and laugh a little bit," Stoops said. "But I love it. I love the fact that he was there and is still concerned and cares about the program ... . I believe people earn their way. And he has."

Which brings us back to that poster with Wilkinson, Switzer and Stoops. Some say Stoops is on his way to earning that recognition, as well.

"Hopefully, by the time I'm finished coaching here, I'll have more in common with those guys than my first name starting with a 'B,' " Stoops said. "Hopefully, we'll be able to win in the same way. It seems to be happening, but I'm not so sure it's because my name begins with a 'B.'

"It's a decent start, that's for sure. You need to continue it. But I'm excited about that, too."

HEUPEL'S DREAM IN AUGUST BECAME REALITY IN JANUARY

By George Schroeder
The Daily Oklahoman, Jan. 1, 2001

ONE SWELTERING afternoon last August, Josh Heupel gathered his teammates. The Oklahoma Sooners had just finished a lackluster practice. Two-a-days were grinding on; the Sooners were wearing down. Heupel didn't like what he sensed.

In a meeting room inside the Barry Switzer Center, the normally emotionless quarterback delivered an emotional exhortation. His voice rose, then cracked. His eyes misted. His teammates took notice.

This was Heupel's message: "We can win every game we play."

A few days from the start of the season — and one season removed from three consecutive losing seasons — Heupel proclaimed the Sooners a legitimate national title contender.

"It was his dream," senior linebacker Roger Steffen said. "Something you could see was from the heart. He wasn't just up there giving a speech. It wasn't just a little pep talk. It was something he believed in.

"And he made everybody else in the room believe along with him."

Looking back, senior defensive tackle Jeremy Wilson-Guest said, it's apparent that was a pivotal moment in OU's improbable journey to the Orange Bowl.

"That's really where this whole season started," Wilson-Guest said.

This is where it ends. More than four months and 12 victories later, here is Heupel's dream, teetering on the edge of reality.

With a perfect season and the national championship at stake, this is his teammates' answer, by now a full-throated roar: We believe.

Forget Florida State, which is ranked No. 3 by the AP but No. 2 in the all-important Bowl Championship Series ratings, is a $10\frac{1}{2}$-point favorite for tonight's matchup at Pro Player Stadium. Forget the bookmakers and many in the media don't give the Sooners much of a chance.

If anything, that will serve as added incentive for a team that said it needs no more motivation than the opportunity to complete a remarkable rise from the ash heap to the pinnacle of college football.

"We're the University of Oklahoma," junior receiver Josh Norman said. "We've got six national championships here, 37 conference championships. It's not just by chance that we're 12-0 and competing for the national championship. People can say what they say."

Like most college football fans, many of these Sooners watched a year ago as Florida State drop-kicked Virginia Tech in the Sugar Bowl. Fresh off an Independence Bowl loss to Ole Miss, the Sooners were realistic.

"I don't think I was thinking we'd be in it," Heupel said of watching the national title game.

Said senior free safety J.T. Thatcher: "I really didn't imagine it. I never thought I'd be playing for a national championship."

But sometime during the winter and spring, as the Sooners reflected on some of their come-from-ahead losses in 1999, and noticed the results from an increased commitment to conditioning, something emerged: an increased confidence, a growing sense of what could be.

Some players dared to think big. Some confided in their closest friends their thoughts. But until Heupel dared come forward in August, most of those ideas remained whispers.

"I think most of us knew we could win every game," senior defensive tackle Ryan Fisher said. "Josh just kind of brought it before everybody else in case they didn't. It helped everybody else on the team believe, too."

And if the Sooners didn't quite understand when the quarterback spoke, they grasped Heupel's meaning sometime along the way.

"It all kind of snowballed," Fisher said.

Maybe it was at the Cotton Bowl, when the Sooners buried the Texas Longhorns — and the first OU oranges cascaded onto a football field. Or at Manhattan, Kan., when they buried a heavy favorite on its home field.

Maybe it was two weeks later. As a slightly startled nation watched, the Sooners stunned No. 1 Nebraska with 31 straight points and wrested away the Huskers' top ranking.

"In that stretch in October, your confidence is growing in a big way," Coach Bob Stoops said. "Win the way we did, that will boost your confidence."

The finish wasn't as pretty. But wins over Texas A&M, Texas Tech and Oklahoma State were wins. And in each of those games, the Sooners found a way to make plays.

The biggest might have come in College Station, Texas, when Torrance Marshall's fourth-quarter interception return for a touchdown propelled the Sooners to victory and persuaded many that old Sooner Magic had returned.

"You get to expecting it," Stoops said. "You get 100 guys that really believe something good is going to happen, it usually does.

"And our guys have that feeling."

For the last month, since winning the Big 12 championship, and especially for the last nine days in South Florida, the Sooners have been confronted with the enormous spotlight and hoopla that accompanies the national title game.

"I don't think anybody is in awe," senior fullback Seth Littrell said. "It's very new to us. We have not been to a national championship game. It's a big place. ... But I don't think anything is going to surprise us. We've handled it well all year, and I think we'll continue handling it well."

Said Coach Bob Stoops: "It's not overwhelming to anybody. Our guys can't wait to play the game."

Several times, Heupel has been reminded of the question he asked Stoops during his recruiting visit to OU, just more than two years ago now.

"Can we win a Big 12 championship and the national championship while I'm here?" the quarterback asked.

Stoops nodded.

"Yes," he told the junior-college player. "I believe we can, provided you're everything we think you are."

Heupel said Stoops' confident air sold him.

"He was able to sell his vision, more than anything," Heupel said. "That's key. There are a lot of ways to win, but the most important thing is to get kids to buy into your vision."

Two years later, the Sooners say they believe. And the national title is within reach because the Sooners bought into Heupel's preseason vision.

"You see your leader, the guy that's going to have to lead you to wherever you go, you see him get emotionally involved — you could tell he really meant it and believed that we could get there," Wilson-Guest said.

—— OU ——

SOONER FANS CHEER RETURNING OU HEROES

By Ed Godfrey and Robert Medley
The Daily Oklahoman, Jan. 4, 2001

T HE NATIONAL championship University of Oklahoma football team returned home to Norman tonight to an enthusiastic welcome from thousands of Sooner fans who waited patiently for more than two hours outside Oklahoma Memorial Stadium. The Sooners, who beat Florida State, 13-2, in the Orange Bowl Wednesday night, appeared on a balcony at team headquarters above a frenzied crowd of supporters. Players pointed camcorders and led cheers.

OU quarterback Josh Heupel led the crowd in two verses of a homemade version of Florida State's "tomahawk chop" chant.

"Ok-la-homa, Ok-la-homa," the quarterback sang, terming it a "new little version" of the Seminole battle cry the team became all too familiar with during its trip to Florida

Coach Bob Stoops also took a shot at cheerleading, spurring the crowd in chants of "We're Number One! We're Number One!"

Waving and holding red-and-white balloons, the crowd spilled out of the plaza outside the Barry Switzer Center and across the street.

Fans lined up on both side of Jenkins Avenue outside the stadium to greet the team. It was a sea of color and noise, with fans shouting, "OU No. 1," carrying flags and signs, and singing "Boomer Sooner."

The flood of fans eventually forced Jenkins to be cordoned off for the massive street party.

Sooners aren't known for patience. The name itself suggests otherwise. The original Sooners were claim jumpers — settlers unwilling to wait for the official Land Run openings of the unassigned lands.

However, two hours standing in the cold was nothing for these fans. They brought their children to wait with them. They brought their video cameras to capture every moment to show their appreciation.

They had been patient for 15 years. It had been that long since their Sooners had won a national football title.

While that may not qualify as long-suffering at most schools, it does at OU, where conference and national championships are almost considered a birthright.

Fifteen years was a long and torturous wait, but now it is over and Sooner fans are rejoicing.

Without a complaint, they cheered and chanted "We're No. 1" until the Sooner players arrived. When the players finally returned home, they were greeted like heroes.

Stoops told the approximately 2,000 fans in attendance that "all of you are part of the national championship.

"It's great to be back in Norman with our great fans and it's great to know that OU football's back," Stoops said, before turning a microphone over to his players.

Safety J.T. Thatcher, who experienced two losing seasons with the Sooners in 1997 and 1998, thanked the crowd for sticking with the team through less heady times.

After a plane carrying the team landed at the Oklahoma City airport at 7 p.m., the Sooners boarded five identical buses — surrounded by eight highway patrol cruisers — for the 20-mile trip to the University of Oklahoma campus. Heupel rode in a patrol car.

Fans were discouraged from going to the airport because of

transportation concerns, but a few dozen people turned out there to catch a glimpse of the new national champions. The real party was at team headquarters. "This is unbelievable," Calmus said of the crowd. "You all are truly the best fans in America."

The national championship is something that Jack Shoopman, 48, of Norman, doubted he would ever see as the Sooners suffered through mediocre seasons for most of the decade.

"I didn't think we would ever return to the prominence we once held," Shoopman said

Bernadean Roper, 70, of Oklahoma City, sat shivering in the cold outside the stadium, waiting for the Sooners to arrive. Roper graduated from OU in 1974, which was another national championship season.

Kim Gilchrist, 41, of Norman, said her city was a madhouse today.

This whole town is booming — the flags, the horns," she said. "The fans are buying everything they can get their hands on."

On an evening much warmer than the day the Sooners' airplane departed an icy runway for Miami, a crowd of Sooner fans jockeyed to get a glimpse of the national champions at Will Rogers World Airport.

Former OU student Cyndi Jennings, 30, waited at the airport to take a flight home to Greenville, S.C. Her Orange Bowl ticket was on the 25-yard line. She wore the same OU Orange Bowl sweatshirt she wore at the game. Jennings and her husband, Jake, have followed the Sooners all their lives.

"It (the season) has been an inspiration. It was something unexpected, like a gift," Cyndi Jennings said.

As the crowd outside the terminal grew before the arrival, airport security kept non-ticket-holders from entering Concourse B.

Standing outside, brothers Sean and Jason Carl of Wheatland waited to see the players board the buses.

"When I bleed, I bleed crimson," Jason Carl said.

The Wal-Mart sporting goods salesman said he was thrilled by the Sooner victory.

"When I woke up this morning, I said, 'Did it happen?' I had to go to the VCR to watch it. It did."

STOOPS ADDS COACH OF THE YEAR HONORS

By *The Associated Press*
The Daily Oklahoman, Jan. 11, 2001

P HOENIX — Oklahoma's youthful coach Bob Stoops won the Eddie Robinson/FWAA Coach of the Year Award given annually to the top coach in Division I-A football during a banquet on tonight at The Phoenician Resort.

Stoops, 40, who directed the Sooners to the 2000 national championship during his second year at the school, won the award after a month-long balloting by the Football Writers Association of America. The FWAA has presented a coaching award since 1957. But Stoops is the first Oklahoma coach to win the award.

The gala banquet was hosted by Fox Sports Net's Kevin Frazier and Kellen Winslow. A premiere telecast will take place on most FSN networks across the country Friday, Jan. 12, at 7:30 p.m. local time (check local listings). FWAA president Dave Sittler of the Tulsa World presented Stoops the bust of Robinson. Stoops beat out Oregon State coach Dennis Erickson and Louisville coach John L. Smith for the award.

Legendary Grambling State University Coach Eddie Robinson, the winningest coach in college football history, was on hand at the banquet for the announcement of the winner. During his 55-year coaching career, Robinson amassed 408 wins and led Grambling to 17 Southwestern Athletic Conference titles, nine black college national championships and had a streak of 27 consecutive winning seasons from 1960-1986.

Earlier this week, Stoops was named the American Football Coaches Associations Coach of the Year during their annual meeting in Atlanta.

The award is the only coach of the year award voted on by coaches.

It took Stoops just two seasons to return the Sooners to national prominence in claiming their seventh national championship. The Sooners were the only team to finish the 2000 regular season with an undefeated record, with several impressive victories along the way. They defeated Florida State, 13-2, in the FedEx Orange Bowl on Jan. 3 to win the Sooners' first national title in 15 years.

The Sooners capped their unblemished run through the regular season with a 27-24 victory over Kansas State in the Big 12 championship. Stoops guided OU to wins over No. 2 Kansas State and No. 1 Nebraska in consecutive weeks, marking the first time in NCAA history that one program has beaten the top two ranked teams in back-to-back games.

In just 25 games, Stoops won the hearts of Sooner fans across the country by leading OU to its first back-to-back winning seasons since 1990-91, consecutive bowl appearances since 1993-94 and the top spot in both national polls. Stoops engineered his own brand of football once he took over at Oklahoma, changing the offense, defense and special teams.

Oklahoma enters the national championship game with a 12-game winning streak, the longest in major college football. It's the first-ever 13-0 season for the Sooners and their first conference title since 1987. Offensively, OU ended the regular season ranked 13th nationally in total offense, ninth in passing and eighth in scoring. On defense, Oklahoma held the 18th best scoring defense in the nation.

STOOPS SAYS HE'LL STAY AT OKLAHOMA

By George Schroeder
The Daily Oklahoman, Jan. 13, 2001

NORMAN — Oklahoma coach Bob Stoops defused speculation about his future this afternoon. Stoops told a nearly packed house at the Lloyd Noble Center he intends to be OU's head football coach for "a long time."

"I want to let everybody know that I still believe it's a privilege to be the head football coach at Oklahoma," Stoops said to thunderous applause during halftime of the OU-Kansas basketball game. "We've got the very best administration in the country. We've got the best fans in the country. I'm fortunate I've got the very best assistant coaches in the country and I get to coach the best players in the country.

"With all that being said, regardless of what you hear, I plan on being at Oklahoma for a long time."

At a press conference moments later, Stoops reiterated the point. But he would not address questions regarding his potential interest in the Cleveland Browns' vacant head-coaching position or whether he had been contacted by the Browns.

"I'm not getting into any of that," Stoops said. "That's

something that's personal. Whether I did or not, or whether I will ever or whatnot, doesn't need to be discussed or hashed around any more. In my life right now, I'm fortunate to be the head football coach here.

"Hopefully they'll have me here for quite a while. I plan on that. Life's never certain of anything, but right now I believe I've got the best football job in the country, and that means college or pros."

In Friday's edition of The Tulsa World, Stoops said he is "intrigued" by the idea of coaching in the NFL and said he would be interested in talking to the Browns if they called.

"I said it intrigues me," Stoops said Saturday. "A lot of things intrigue me. Coaching high school intrigues me. ... I don't think you ever say never to anything. That's a long time. You never know from year to year what your life brings you or what you want out of it."

Browns president Carmen Policy is from Stoops' hometown of Youngstown, Ohio, and is a longtime acquaintance. Stoops told the newspaper Policy had left messages on his voice-mail earlier in the week.

Athletic director Joe Castiglione said Stoops told him he had not been contacted by Browns officials. Stoops declined to reveal whether he had to choose between OU and Cleveland.

"That's not fair to them or me to get into particulars about any of it," he said.

It's the second time in less than two weeks Stoops has been linked to an Ohio coaching vacancy. A day before the Orange Bowl, when Ohio State fired coach John Cooper, Stoops was immediately mentioned as a top candidate. A day after the Orange Bowl, Stoops said he would not talk to Ohio State if contacted.

When the Browns fired coach Chris Palmer Thursday, Policy had glowing praise for Stoops' accomplishments. But Stoops comments to The Tulsa World ignited the controversy.

In a statement, OU president David Boren said he was "pleased that Bob Stoops has reaffirmed his clear decision to stay at OU." Castiglione said he is confident Stoops will not talk with Cleveland. He said he believes Stoops put the issue to rest.

"He expressed what he wanted on the subject, and that's good enough for me," Castiglione said. "He told me it's not about any of that, it's about his affirmation of being the head coach at the University of Oklahoma. I think it's a moot issue. There's really no story other than the fact that there's an affirmation of him here as our coach. That says it all."

Stoops said he decided to make a public statement because of the brewing speculation.

"It got to this point, I needed to say this is what I intend to do," Stoops said.

A couple hours earlier, Stoops had delivered a similar message to a group of 13 recruits and their families making an official visit to OU. Stoops said the timing did not hurt the Sooners' recruiting effort.

"It hasn't affected recruiting one bit. In fact, it enhances it," Stoops said. "I think all those recruits recognize when that happens and particularly when the NFL is calling that this staff is a quality staff.

"It only hurts it if you leave, and I don't intend to do that."

Stoops recently signed a contract extension worth $1.4 million annually through the 2005 season. OU officials believe the contract ranks among the top four in college football. With incentives, Stoops will make $1.957 million this year.

The contract includes a buyout clause equal to one year's base salary — $200,000. If Stoops leaves before Dec. 1, he must also repay a $200,000 signing bonus.

Stoops could make significantly more money in the NFL. Castiglione didn't rule out another salary increase — "we'll keep that amongst ourselves," he said — but said OU's stance toward compensation of coaches has been "proactive."

"Our whole approach has been to keep things ahead of us so when these types of situations develop that we aren't sitting here trying to figure out what we're going to do," Castiglione said. "We try to do all of this well in advance."

STOOPS GUIDES THE LOST SOONER NATION BACK TO THE PROMISED LAND

By Barry Tramel and George Schroeder
The Daily Oklahoman, Jan. 14, 2001

NORMAN — Bob Stoops woke the giant with a firm kick and a stout voice.

Get up, let's go. Games to play, titles to win.

The giant — the monster called Oklahoma football — shook off slumber, threw water on its face and hurried to catch stride with the self-assured coach already off to conquer college football.

"When he first got here, he said, 'we're not waiting around,' " OU flanker Andre Woolfolk said.

Today, the giant, two years awake, roars with its seventh national championship and Stoops sits on its shoulders, navigating sure steps that not so long ago staggered.

"The way he does things, the way he goes about things, it's infectious," said Matt McMillen, Stoops' administrative assistant and close friend.

Infected. That's what happened to Oklahoma football 25 months ago. The Sooners were infected with confidence, courtesy of a wizard who waved not a wand but an attitude. The fever spread, slowly at first, but finally it bubbled to the point where Oklahoma felled a fellow giant, Florida State, 13-2, in the Orange Bowl on Jan. 3.

One day in Miami, Bob Stoops sat poolside with a good portion of his coaching staff.

Mark Mangino was there. Mike Stoops, too. Steve Spurrier Jr. Chuck Long. McMillen. They sat around laughing and relaxing at the Miami Airport Marriott.

It was game day. The afternoon of the Orange Bowl.

"That's the way the whole day was," McMillen said. "No different than Arkansas State.

"I think the players really watch him, take his lead. He doesn't get upset. The bus might be late, but he never makes anything into a big deal."

Stoops is not a laid-back coach. Far from it. Just ask the OU defensive backs he reems out in practice or the Big 12 officials he accosts after a crucial call.

Stoops is a matter-of-fact coach. In control of himself. Stoops sets a tone and is unassailable. He never cracks, or at least is getting to that point. He displays absolute confidence.

His preferred kickoff time is whenever kickoff is. His preferred playing surface is whichever surface the Sooners are playing on.

The most mundane tasks aren't met with complaints. Stoops just sits down and does them.

"Those players read you like a book every day," he said. "It's a big part of my job. They're constantly studying you.

"If you get to feeling too good about being No. 1 in the sixth or seventh game of the year, then they will. They are going to play off what your attitude is."

It's coachspeak and it's cliché and it's frankly tiresome to hear. But darned if it didn't work in 2000, when the Sooners ran the gauntlet — 13 straight wins — and had only two games decided by single digits.

Stoops sat in the Florida locker room a few years ago and

wondered about the football program on the plains where, in 1979, he made his college playing debut.

"I remember thinking, how can a team like Oklahoma not be competing?" Stoops said. "It's a sleeping giant."

When Stoops arrived in December 1998, the Sooners had just finished their third straight losing year. The two years before that were both .500 seasons. The five-year slump: 23-33-1. The giant snored.

"I was surprised when I walked in at the lack of expectation and almost neglecting our tradition and history," Stoops said. "I don't know if it was the fear of living up to it or whatnot, but we needed to change that."

Stoops showed such confidence during the interview process.

OU athletic director Joe Castiglione met Stoops in Dallas for the first of two interviews and came away thinking, "He was going to be hard to beat."

Castiglione meant for the job. Turns out the same holds true on the football field.

There always is trepidation when hiring an assistant coach to run a program. There usually is tremendous upside (Bud Wilkinson and Barry Switzer) but massive downside (Gomer Jones and John Blake). With an established head coach, schools usually know what they're getting.

But Stoops was a little different. He had coached for Hayden Fry, Bill Snyder and Steve Spurrier, three of the best program-builders of the last quarter century. At Florida, he was more than the defensive coordinator; Stoops virtually was head coach/defense.

"My dad was the offensive coordinator," said Spurrier Jr., who was on the Florida staff with Stoops and followed him to Oklahoma. "He didn't know what the defense was doing. He said, 'they're yours. I don't understand what you're doing, just take care of it.' "

Castiglione thus encountered a young, sharp coach with the best of bloodlines who said all the right things and, even better, said them in the best of ways. Natural.

"What I wanted to see in a leader," Castiglione said. "He was well-prepared to step into this role. Maybe more so than what one would expect from an assistant coach. I really felt confident he

Bob Stoops (80) jumps on a teammate after the Cardinal Mooney High Cardinals had scored a touchdown.

Stoops was a star linebacker at Cardinal Mooney High School.

Ron Stoops (top right) and his family in Youngstown, Ohio.

Stoops (41) was named Iowa's Most Valuable Player in 1982. He finished his career with the Hawkeyes with 205 total tackles and 10 interceptions.

Stoops was a 4-year starter for the Iowa Hawkeyes. Twice, he was named All-Big Ten at defensive back and in 1982 was an honorable mention all-American selection.

Stoops (second row, fourth from left) joined Bill Snyder's staff at Kansas State in 1989. Serving as the defensive coordinator for five of his seven seasons there, the Wildcats went from being a perennial loser to becoming a bigtime winner in the Big 12 Conference.

University of Florida coach Steve Spurrier hired Stoops in 1996 to serve as his defensive coordinator. The Gators won the National Championship in 1996 and two SEC titles during Stoops' three-year tenure in Gainesville.

The Stoops siblings with their mother, Dee (center) on a family vacation. (left to right) Mike, Bob, Renee, Dee, Kathy, Mark and Ronnie.

Stoops speaks to a crowd after being introduced as the Sooners' new head football coach in December 1998.

The Stoops family at 1999 OU football media day. (left to right) His wife, Carol, holding son Drake, and Issac and Mackenzie on their dad's knee.

Stoops dresses up as the Sooners' new sheriff prior to the 1999 season.

Above, Stoops signs autographs during media day in 1999. *Right,* The Sooners' coach protests a call with an official during the 1999 Iowa State game.

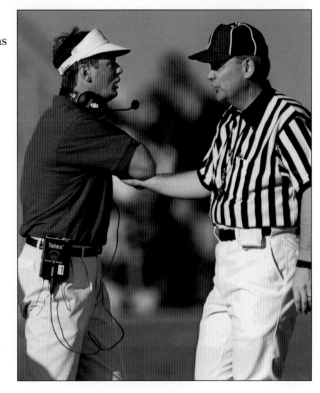

OU's new coach observes practice along with the kids at his Sooner
Football Camp in 1999.

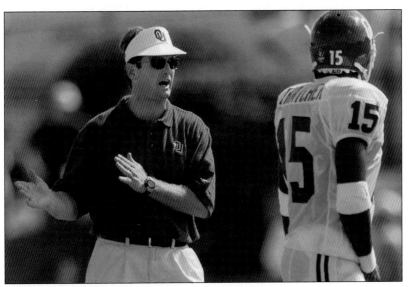

Stoops talks with defensive back and punt returner J.T. Thatcher
during a scrimmage in Tulsa in 1999.

On the sidelines against Indiana State during his first game as a Sooners coach in 1999. Stoops' OU squad defeated the Sycamores, 49-0.

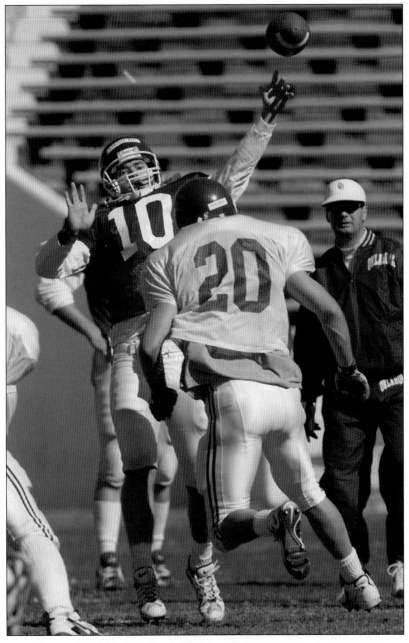

Stoops watches as quarterback Josh Heupel (10) gets a pass off before linebacker Rocky Calmus can touch him during a scrimmage in 1999.

The roof of the home of Dr. Jim and Mary Kay Burkett of Oklahoma City leaves no doubt as to their feelings about OU's new head football coach.

Stoops speaks to the press before an Independence Bowl luncheon in Shreveport, La., in December 1999.

After the Sooners defeated Oklahoma State, 44-7, in 1999, Stoops gets doused with a bucket of water by tight end Trent Smith (88).

Above, Dave Sittler presents the Eddie Robinson/FWAA Coach of the Year award to Stoops. *Below,* (left to right) Kevin Keleghan of Sears, Josh Heupel, Stoops, Torrence Marshall and Orange Bowl President Sherill Hudson, pose with the BCS National Championship trophy.

Soph Damian Mackey (13) darts through the FSU secondary.

Quentin Griffin scores a fourth-quarter touchdown against FSU.

Josh Heupel attempts a pass against Florida State in the 2001 Orange Bowl as Frank Romero (63) blocks the Seminoles' Jamal Reynolds.

Above, Josh Heupel receives the Walter Camp Award from Walter Camp Football Foundation Bernard Pellegrino. Stoops was also named the foundation's College Coach of the Year. *Below,* Stoops and the OU team, with their championship trophies on hand, are given a standing ovation during halftime at the 2001 Oklahoma-Kansas basketball game.

possessed all the right qualifications, personally and professionally."

Stoops' confidence drew national raves in the glare of the Orange Bowl. But his assembly of a vibrant coaching staff was recognized almost immediately in national circles.

Stoops' first offensive coordinator, Mike Leach, was hired to coach at Texas Tech a year ago. His second, Mangino, won the Broyles Award this weekend as the nation's top assistant coach. Co-defensive coordinators Mike Stoops and Brent Venables were cornerstones of Kansas State's remarkable surge, and their unit's play in the Orange Bowl was historic.

"First and foremost, he treats us very well," said quarterback coach Chuck Long, hired in December 1999. "He's very professional in what he does. He's very demanding and yet he understands what an assistant coach goes through."

The 40-year-old Stoops was an assistant coach for 16 years. He coached for a variety of personalities. Fry, the raw-boned Texan. Snyder, the unrelenting taskmaster who never lets down his guard. Spurrier, the self-assured genius who never puts up his guard.

Stoops spent those years studying not just football but the personalities of the game. He knew what kind of program and staff he wanted.

He continually deflects praise toward his staff. More telling, he has no bridles on his coaches. While Stoops is very calculated in his public comments, he doesn't demand that his coaches follow that lead.

Bob Stoops said he spends a lot of thought on what his players are thinking, what the tone of the game is, what newspapers will write, what his players will read and "all I need to combat it to make sure they have the right mental frame going into the game."

"He's definitely the type of person that makes you want to associate with him," Spurrier Jr. said of Stoops. "You want to follow him. You believe what he's saying. He's got an air about him that makes everyone around him very confident.

"And winning helps."

STOOPS WINS BEAR BRYANT AWARD

By Mike Lutz
The Associated Press, Jan. 17, 2001

HOUSTON — Bob Stoops, the Oklahoma coach who led the Sooners to the national championship in only his second season at the school, received the Bear Bryant Award tonight as the top college football coach.

Stoops was selected from a field of six finalists in voting by the National Sportscasters and Sportswriters Association. Other finalists were Florida State's Bobby Bowden, South Carolina's Lou Holtz, Oregon State's Dennis Erickson, Miami's Butch Davis and Dennis Franchione, who was at Texas Christian before moving to Alabama.

The Sooners finished 13-0 and beat Florida State, 13-2, in the Orange Bowl for the school's first national title since 1985.

THE
1999 SEASON

STOOPS ERA STARTS WITH WHIPPING OF INDIANA STATE

By Mac Bentley
The Daily Oklahoman, Sept. 11, 1999

NORMAN — The Bob Stoops era got off to a clean start Saturday night.

Oklahoma got everything it could out of a Division I-AA opponent, slapping around little Indiana State 49-0 before a big crowd (74,119) at Memorial Stadium.

The Sooners did just about everything right, with the obvious exception of four turnovers. Records were set and tied by the offense, namely Josh Heupel, who completed 31 of 40 passes for 341 yards and five touchdowns.

The defense was close enough to dominating that it needs no excuses for a few lapses against a triple-option offense.

There were plenty of reasons to be pleased with this win, which despite the Sycamore's I-AA status helps in Oklahoma's search for its first bowl trip since 1994. But the real judgments will have to wait until the Sooners play Baylor, Louisville and Notre Dame over the next three weeks.

"I realize we're going to meet stronger opponents," said Stoops. "Indiana State is a good, solid I-AA program coached very well. They were just outmanned. We recognize that."

Perhaps the most startling statistic coming out of the opener was in the penalty column: one for the Sooners, for 10 yards. It came on an illegal, below-the-waist block early in the second quarter. Penalties have been a major concern with the Sooners over the past several years, a concern that carried into the first $3^1/_2$ weeks of fall practices.

"I felt great about the discipline of the players, the execution throughout the game," said Stoops, who is now 1-0 as a head coach. "I think we had one penalty through the entire day. The triple-option takes great discipline to keep it out of the end zone.

"I felt great about the attitude and preparation going into the game. It was a I-AA team, still (we were) ready to play. Anytime you're excited about going out to play you have a great chance."

During his record-setting night, Heupel had one interception. Even that one wasn't his fault, Stoops said.

"The receivers did a poor job, bumped each other off," he said.

The 31 completions broke the school record of 25 set by Cale Gundy, now the Sooners' running backs coach, in the 48-14 victory over Virginia in the 1991 Gator Bowl.

The five TD passes broke the school record of four, which had been accomplished four times in the past. Claude Arnold did it twice in 1950, Eddie Crowder did it in 1951 and Eric Moore threw for four against Kansas State in 1996.

The 341 passing yards by Heupel tied a Gundy record set in 1992 with a 22-of-28 performance against Texas Tech.

"It was something special to come out for your first game and I thought we played pretty well tonight," said Heupel. "The one thing you don't concern yourself with is breaking records, throws or completions, you're just trying to move the ball and it's really insignificant how you do it."

"He never had a delay of game, checked out of a good number of plays with good selections, really was solid throughout the game," Stoops said of Heupel. "He had a solid night."

The crowd was the Sooners' largest since the Louisville game two years ago, and the largest for a season-opener since Arizona visited in 1988.

While the offensive starters were in the game, which was up until the final 10 minutes, the Sooners scored touchdowns on seven of 13 possessions. They punted twice and lost three fumbles, two by Jarrail Jackson on his first two pass receptions of the night.

The other fumble was coughed up by Michael Thornton at the Indiana State 2-yard line with 12:49 remaining. The interception came on a second-and-8 from the ISU 17-yard line as Heupel was picked off by DeJuan Alfonzo, a cornerback who received All-American recognition at the Division I-AA level last season.

"Obviously we're not going to be able to win in the Big 12 with four turnovers, so that's the one spot we've got to improve on," said Stoops. "We've got to be able to take care of the football. Hopefully that's just a first-time-out thing."

INDIANA STATE	0	0	0	0	—	0
OKLAHOMA	14	14	14	7	—	49

HEUPEL SETS MORE RECORDS AS OU BASHES BAYLOR

By Mac Bentley
The Daily Oklahoman, Sept. 18, 1999

NORMAN — The plot thickened at Memorial Stadium today.

The burning question around these parts — how good are the Sooners? — wasn't answered in a 41-10, Big 12 victory over the Baylor Bears.

Oklahoma still hasn't been challenged, at least not to an extent that tips the scales enough for an accurate reading. Except for a couple of lapses, the Sooners were in complete command of their second straight lopsided victory on Owen Field before another sellout crowd (74,309).

This much they've shown in their first two games: Oklahoma is way too good for a Division I-AA team, and considerably better than their first Division I-A foe, Baylor, which they'd beaten the past three years by a total of 17 points.

The Sooners again had 30 first downs and more than 500 total yards, handling the 0-3 Bears just about as easily as OU handled Indiana State in a 49-0 victory a week ago.

"I think the course of the Big 12 season will show how good a football team we are," said quarterback Josh Heupel. "We expect ourselves to be a very good football team. We expect to do things a lot better than we did today."

The Sooners will learn more on upcoming road trips to Louisville and Notre Dame, but those concerns are better left to another day. For now, they'll celebrate being 1-0 in the Big 8/12 for the first time since 1994.

Oklahoma played well enough that Coach Bob Stoops wasn't interested in dwelling on negatives, at least not right off the bat in his post-game press conference.

Concerned with the early penalties? he was asked.

"Aw come on, first question out of the box? When you win, 41-10, I won't worry about it," he said.

He'll worry about it in due time, of course, but there were too many good things to talk about after this one.

Heupel had another record-setting performance, hitting 37 of 54 passes for 420 yards and three touchdowns, with two interceptions.

The 37 completions broke the single-game record he set a week ago, and the 420 yards shattered the previous record of 341 yards, which he shared with Cale Gundy. His 54 attempts and 397 yards of total offense also set records.

The Sooners drove 57, 80 and 94 yards for touchdowns to break open a 21-0 lead, were a bit slugging in the second quarter, then dominated the second half with the exception of a defensive lapse in the fourth quarter allowing Baylor an 83-yard, 9-play drive for its only touchdown.

"It's a good situation when you can go into your locker room after winning, 41-10, and in the Big 12 Conference, and none of the players are overly excited," said Stoops. "We realize we can play so much better. Our players certainly recognize that there are a lot of positives in this game and that we did a lot of things well to be able to win the way we did.

"Still, our players are hungry to play to their potential and play the best they can. We want to get them there, and it's frustrating because we still feel we can play so much better and eliminate some of the bad plays that we had, so we're going to keep pushing for that."

Heupel's interceptions both came in the first half under duress from the Baylor defense. And after being flagged just once last week, the Sooners were whistled for five penalties in the first quarter alone, finishing with 11 for 90 yards.

And in the third period, Jarrail Jackson, the usually sure-handed receiver and punt returner, followed up last week's two-fumble performance with back-to-back muffs of punts, one of which was lost to the Bears.

Oklahoma also had two touchdowns and a 70-yard gain nullified by penalties.

"Great job by Josh Heupel of finding the right receivers, great job of the line and backs protecting him, did a super job picking up their stunts," said Stoops. "Josh gets a lot of help out there and he's doing an excellent job. Hopefully he learned something today in a way that really doesn't hurt us.

"He was careless a few times with the ball, extremely careless in a couple of situations that hopefully he'll learn from. He's still gaining experience."

Baylor was held to 208 yards total offense, 157 of that coming through the air. The Bears had the ball in OU territory four times in the first half, but could come away with only a 35-yard field goal by Kyle Atteberry. They had a minus-2 yards of offense over their first three possessions of the second half before the TD drive.

"That was a pretty rough one to swallow," said Baylor coach Kevin Steele. "They executed their new offense very well and their quarterback played very well for them. That offense is one where you have to match up on their receivers and play one on one and bring as much pressure on the quarterback to get the ball out of his hands.

"We came in with that philosophy but we didn't hold up ... It was a physical whipping, not so much as the three yards and a cloud of dust kind of physical, I mean they executed better than we executed by a large degree."

BAYLOR	0	3	0	7	—	10
OKLAHOMA	14	7	3	17	—	41

OU

LET HEUPEL HYPE BEGIN: SOONERS AIRMAIL CARDINALS

By Mac Bentley
The Daily Oklahoman, Sept. 15, 1999

LOUISVILLE, KY. — Oklahoma's defense gave up 386 yards, 17 first downs and 21 points to Louisville today.

The Sooners wouldn't have dared hope for better.

"No one's going to hold them to 50 (passing) yards in the second half," OU coach Bob Stoops said. "No one's going to keep them under 300 (passing) yards. I want to see it if you do."

He saw it today from his own club, though, as the Sooners tempered Chris Redman's Heisman hopes in a 42-21 victory over the Cardinals before 41,214 fans at Papa John's Cardinal Stadium.

OU quarterback Josh Heupel threw for a school-record 429 yards and five touchdowns and ran for another. Meanwhile, Redman was held to 77 yards in the second half while hitting eight of 20 passes.

"That is hard to do," Stoops said. "He's (Redman) as good a quarterback as I've seen in a long time."

The Sooners, 3-0 for the first time since 1995, trailed 3-0 early in the second quarter, 10-7 later in the quarter, 13-7 at the half and 21-14 midway through the third period, but then outscored the

Cardinals, 28-0, to pick up their third victory of the season and fifth straight dating back to last year.

The Oklahoma offense scored more than 40 points and had more than 500 total yards (544) for the third straight game.

While Redman was connecting on just 48.9 percent (24-of-49) of his passes and averaging 5.9 yards per attempt, Oklahoma southpaw Josh Heupel was hitting 69 percent (29-of-42) and averaging 10.2 per attempt.

Heupel passed for 429 yards, raising his own school record, and threw five touchdown passes to equal his own school mark set in the opener.

The Sooner defense really began taking charge in the second quarter. Three of Louisville's possessions in the period began at the OU 38, 19 and 38, thanks to a Heupel interception, a Heupel fumble on a sack and a shanked punt by Jeff Ferguson.

But the Cardinals got only six points out of the three gifts, field goals of 27 and 35 yards by Jon Hilbert.

"They gave us a lot of things to look at," said Louisville coach John L. Smith. "The further we got down in there, (they were) bringing things, they did a good job. They had answers and we didn't. We've got to come up with a few."

One of the answers the Sooner defense had was tipping and knocking down passes at the line of scrimmage. Six of Redman's incompletions were deflected by OU linemen — three by Ramon Richardson, two by Bary Holleyman and one by Cornelius Burton.

"We emphasized that all week, we knew they liked to throw the ball quick and that was part of our plan, get three-step and get our hands up and knock 'em down," defensive coordinator Mike Stoops said. "That was a big point of emphasis all week. We were ready for his quick game."

In all, the Sooners were credited with 13 break-ups.

Heupel threw passes to eight different receivers and three of them caught the five touchdowns.

Four plays into the third period, the Sooners took a 14-13 lead on a 52-yard scoring play to Jarrail Jackson. This was all pass, though, as Jackson was well-covered when Heupel dropped the ball over his head and into his arms.

Louisville, 2-2, bounced back for a quick 78-yard drive to regain the lead at 21-14 and was looking for more on third-and-one at the OU 38-yard line when safety Rodney Rideau made what Bob Stoops thought may be the play of the game. He intercepted a pass in the end zone that could've put the Cardinals on top, 28-14.

Instead, OU drove 80 yards in seven plays to tie the game on an 11-yard, needle-threading strike to Damien Mackey with 3:20 remaining in the third period.

It was all Oklahoma the rest of the way. On the first play of the fourth quarter, Heupel scrambled and finally found Antwone Savage all alone for a 51-yard gain to the 6-yard line, from where Heupel found Mackey again, this time on a fade.

Heupel scored on his sneak with 9:52 left and then wrapped it up with a 44-yard scoring toss to Jackson with 6:55 remaining. That one came on a fourth-and-1 play in which the Sooners were really trying to draw Louisville offsides.

A Cardinal jumped, Matt O'Neal snapped the ball and, like the 52-yard score to Jackson early in the third, the Sooners scored on a free play.

OKLAHOMA	0	7	14	21	—	42
LOUISVILLE	0	13	8	0	—	21

FIGHTING IRISH SCORE 20 STRAIGHT POINTS, DEFEAT OU

By Mac Bentley
The Daily Oklahoman, Oct. 2, 1999

SOUTH BEND, IND. — Don't give up big plays? Check!

Don't turn the ball over? Check!

Find a way to score in the red zone? Check!

When it came to problem-solving, Notre Dame was a perfect three-for-three this afternoon, snapping its three-game losing streak and halting Oklahoma's season-opening, three-game winning streak.

The Irish, who were oh-for-September, scored the game's final three touchdowns for a come-from-behind, 34-30 victory before another sellout (80,012) at Notre Dame Stadium.

The three tasks mentioned above were expressed during the week by Notre Dame coach Bob Davie as the solution to his club's string of losses to Michigan, Purdue and Michigan State last month. He could have given the Irish one more assignment — dominate — and it would have been four-for-four.

The Sooners, 3-1 and facing Texas next weekend, led, 23-14, at the half and 30-14 less than five minutes into the third quarter. But Notre Dame rallied with touchdown drives of 81, 56 and 98 yards to

110

win its first meeting with Oklahoma in 31 years.

Don't give up big plays? Last week, Oklahoma had four plays of 44 yards or more in a 42-21 victory at Louisville, but today the Sooners' longest play, at least from scrimmage, was a 26-yard touchdown pass from Josh Heupel to Trent Smith.

Don't turn the ball over? Notre Dame didn't. The game's only turnover came in the third quarter when Lee Lafayette intercepted a Heupel pass at the Notre Dame 44. The Irish drove the 56 yards in nine plays to pull within two points at 30-28 with $17\frac{1}{2}$ minutes left in the game.

Find a way to score in the red zone? The Irish scored four touchdowns on six trips inside the 20-yard line. Quarterback Jarious Jackson scored from 10 yards out on a scramble to cap a 76-yard drive less than two minutes in to the game. Notre Dame's other three touchdowns came on a 15-yard pass from Jackson to Jabari Holloway, and a pair of 1-yard dives by Tony Driver, with 2:37 left in the third period and with 9:19 left in the game.

And dominate? The Irish had a 566-237 advantage in total yardage (284-69 in rushing and 282-168 in passing) and a 26-14 advantage in first downs. The Irish offense had the ball for nearly 41 of the game's 60 minutes, averaging 5.1 yards per rushing play and 12.3 yards per passing attempt.

Jackson, the 6-foot-1, 235-pound senior, hit 15 of 21 passes for 276 yards and rushed 15 times for 107 more.

Oklahoma expanded its halftime lead by driving 45 yards after a short Notre Dame punt in the third period. Heupel hit Brandon Daniels with a 15-yard scoring pass and the Sooners appeared headed to victory.

"We were able to move the football consistently all day, so we knew we had a chance," Davie said. "But obviously, I was concerned. We were pushed to the brink right there, which is why I think it was such a significant win."

It was all Notre Dame the rest of the way. The Irish drove 81 yards in nine plays to make it 30-21. Then they drove 56 yards in nine plays to make it 30-28.

Finally, after a Jeff Ferguson punt rolled dead at the Notre Dame

2-yard line, the Irish drove 98 yards in 11 plays. It was suggested to Stoops that perhaps his defense was a bit weary.

"That's their fault," he said. "(You) get off the field when you force a punt, intercept a ball, create a fumble, that's how you get off the field. We've got to play better defense and we won't get as tired."

The defeat spoiled a brilliant performance by the Sooners' Daniels. He had kickoff returns of 89 (for a first-quarter touchdown), 43 and 68 (which set up touchdown drives), 22 and 7 yards. His total of 229 kickoff return yards set a school record.

The Sooners' offense was opportunistic at best. OU's three scoring drives were 37, 26 and 45 yards. After Daniels had tied the score at 7-7 with his 89-yard kickoff return two minutes into the game, his 43- and 68-yard returns set up OU's second and third TDs and the short Notre Dame punt set up the fourth midway through the third period.

The Sooners' other eight possessions all began in their own territory and on only one of those tries did they move into Notre Dame territory.

The Sooners' most dismal effort came at the end of the game. Starting at their own 20 after Notre Dame missed a field goal with 2:21 remaining, Heupel threw four incomplete passes, three of which were dropped by receivers.

OKLAHOMA	7	16	7	0	—	30
NOTRE DAME	7	7	14	6	—	34

OU FALLS TO LONGHORNS FOR THIRD STRAIGHT SEASON

By Mac Bentley
The Daily Oklahoman, Oct. 9, 1999

DALLAS — The idea was for Oklahoma to do like Kansas State: beat Texas by bringing defensive pressure on the quarterback.

Instead, Texas mimicked Notre Dame, beating Oklahoma by hurrying the quarterback, stopping receivers in their tracks and countering the pressure with an opportunistic running game.

Texas' idea worked better, and like the Irish, the Longhorns came from more than two touchdowns behind to defeat the Sooners, 38-28, today in the Cotton Bowl.

Texas erased an early 17-0 Oklahoma lead and led by as many as 11 in the second half on the way to its third straight victory over the Sooners before a 54th consecutive sellout crowd (75,587).

The Sooners could have gotten a big jump on the Big 12 South Division race and appeared quite capable of doing so when they opened a 17-0 lead barely 10 minutes into the game. OU had two touchdowns and a field goal on 172 yards of total offense, averaging 10.8 yards per play.

The Sooners gained just 2.0 yards per play the rest of the half, and 3.1 over the rest of the game as the Longhorns were gaining a 17-17 halftime tie, then outscoring OU, 21-11, in the second half.

The crisp passing game Oklahoma exhibited through its first three games and some of the fourth disappeared in the face of a Texas defense that hurried quarterback Josh Heupel into an uncharacteristic number of poor throws and smothered receivers after completions.

The Longhorns, ranked 23rd in the AP Poll, intercepted three of his passes and recovered a fumbled center-quarterback exchange, although they could only convert three points out of those turnovers.

Texas had turned the ball over six times because of Kansas State pressure in a 35-17 loss last week.

Oklahoma's search for a pass rush was somewhat realized today as Texas quarterback Major Applewhite exhibited a vulnerability, but the Longhorns countered Oklahoma blitzes with a ground game that saw Hodges Mitchell rush for 204 yards on 30 carries. That averages out to 6.8 yards per carry.

OU's leading ball carrier was Michael Thornton, who picked up 25 yards on seven carries, or 3.6 per try.

"This was a game we had to win, not needed to," said Texas coach Mack Brown, whose Horns are 5-2 overall and 2-1 in the Big 12. "I think the offensive line did a great job. We made some big plays on the blitz, and there was not one interception.

"I thought they responded very well."

Oklahoma, once 3-0, fell to 3-2 overall and 1-1 in the Big 12. The Sooners are off this week before hosting Texas A&M on Oct. 23.

"We knew coming in that win or lose this wasn't the end," said Oklahoma coach Bob Stoops. "We need to improve. We have a lot of room to improve."

Texas' only turnover came on a fumble with 4:19 left in the game. OU moved to the Texas 19 before a final interception with 2:59 remaining sealed the Longhorns' largest comeback victory in 34 years.

UT amassed 533 yards of total offense, 225 on the ground and

328 through the air. The Horns outgained OU 322-119 in the second half.

Applewhite passed for more than 300 yards for the fourth time this season, breaking the school record of three times by James Street in 1995.

Applewhite hit 22 of 47 passes for 328 yards and three touchdowns, with no interceptions. Heupel hit 31 of 48 for 311 yards and two touchdowns, with three interceptions.

The Sooners had 13 penalties for 102 yards, but nine of those came in the first half. Texas committed 14 infractions for 125 yards.

OU also converted just two of 12 third-down situations, Texas seven of 18.

A 38-yard kickoff return by Brandon Daniels, an 18-yard pass from Heupel to Thornton and a 44-yard pass to freshman Antwone Savage gave OU a 7-0 lead just 29 seconds into the game.

OU made it 10-0 on a 43-yard field goal by Tim Duncan on their next possession and then drove 71 yards in six plays, with Heupel hitting Jarrail Jackson on a 30-yard touchdown pass, to go up, 17-0, with 4:18 still remaining in the first period.

Texas kicked a field goal late in the first period and two more in the second, then took advantage of Oklahoma's inability to run out the final 1:55 of the first half. Texas covered 61 yards in two plays for the game-tying TD 49 seconds before halftime. Applewhite hit Ryan Nunez on an 11-yard fade for the score.

Texas went on top, 24-17, with an 85-yard, third quarter-opening drive to take the lead for good. OU, taking over at the UT 46 after a 39-yard kickoff return by Daniels, settled for a field goal before Texas made it an 11-point game by driving 80 yards in four plays, the score coming on a 48-yard wide receiver screen pass to Kwame Cavil.

Oklahoma used a little trickery to pull within three points late in the quarter. The Sooners drove from their own 20 to the Texas 4-yard line and appeared ready to kick a field goal on fourth down, but holder Patrick Fletcher, a quarterback, pulled up and threw a TD pass to Duncan for a touchdown.

Heupel then hit Savage for a 2-pointer and it was 31-28.

Texas all but put it away with a 99-yard, 5 $\frac{1}{2}$-minute scoring drive in the fourth quarter. UT converted three third downs on the drive, including a 35-yard pass play on third-and-15 from the OU 49.

OKLAHOMA	17	0	11	0	—	28
TEXAS	3	14	14	7	—	38

OU

STOOPS' TROOPS TOSS AROUND A&M LIKE AG DOLLS

By Mac Bentley
The Daily Oklahoman, Oct. 23, 1999

N ORMAN — Oklahoma had been there before.

Up 17 points in the first quarter ... that was the start of a nightmare the Sooners have carried with them for the two weeks since a 38-28 loss to Texas.

This time, though, it was only the beginning. Oklahoma turned that 17-0 lead into a 34-6 advantage at the half, a 48-6 romp by the end of the third quarter and then a 51-6 victory, the team's biggest in years.

Texas A&M, 13th-ranked in the AP poll and No. 10 in the coaches' poll, was never a factor tonight as the Sooners rolled up 552 total yards against a Wrecking Crew defense ranked eighth nationally.

The Sooners had 30 first downs and ran a whopping 92 offensive plays, 60 of those coming in an explosive first half.

It certainly was one occasion when time of possession, where OU had a 38:29-21:31 advantage, was indicative of the game.

The Sooners, who couldn't cash in on a 16-point lead at Notre Dame and a 17-point lead at Texas, also converted three fourth-down plays, including a fake punt in the first half, in handing the

Aggies their worst defeat in 98 years.

"It was good to play strong in the second half," coach Bob Stoops said. "That was a big emphasis of ours, to come out in the second half and keep the fires burning. Hopefully our players learned from that tonight."

The victory moves Oklahoma to a 4-2 record overall and 2-1 in the Big 12, with a visit to Colorado scheduled next week. Texas A&M drops to 5-2 and 2-2, having also been a homecoming victim at Texas Tech. A third straight sellout crowd of 74,552 in Memorial Stadium saw A&M become the highest-ranked team beaten by the Sooners since these same Aggies, fifth-ranked at the time, get knocked off 44-14 here in the second game of the 1993 season.

This also was OU's first victory over a ranked team since a 30-27, overtime decision over No. 25 Texas in 1996.

"It really wasn't a shoot-out ... we got shot," said A&M coach R.C. Slocum, who had said before the game he didn't want to get into a shoot-out. "We got considerably behind early, to the point we had to throw the ball more than we wanted."

Oklahoma scored the first six times it had the ball and never looked back, apparently having bought into the coaching staff's theme for the past two weeks. The answer to back-to-back losses to Notre Dame and Texas wasn't so much who the Sooners were playing as it was how they were playing.

Only Oklahoma mattered on this night. The Sooners made this lead and made it work.

The momentum they carried out of the locker room cooled only somewhat by the second half, when it took an interception by Roy Williams and three possessions before the Sooners could start putting this one away with the first of two third-quarter touchdowns.

Quarterback Josh Heupel hit 31 of 50 passes for 372 yards and three touchdowns, with one interception. He also scored on three 1-yard sneaks, but was being treated for a shoulder problem after the game.

Michael Thornton caught six of his passes for 62 yards, and Brandon Daniels and Jarrail Jackson caught five apiece, Daniels for 55 yards and Jackson for 32.

Daniels, Curtis Fagan (three for 38) and Trent Smith (3 for 30) caught touchdown passes.

On the ground, Reggie Skinner re-emerged with a 15-carry, 106-yard night. He's Oklahoma's first 100-yard rusher since Thornton went for 110 against Baylor on Sept. 18, the last time OU played on Owen Field.

The victory was the fifth straight at home for the Sooners and snapped a four-game losing streak to the Aggies. They had been beaten by A&M the last two years by a combined, 80-7 score, including 29-0 last year at College Station. OU prevented Slocum from picking up his 100th career win and the Aggies from picking up the program's 600th win.

Aggie quarterback Randy McCown came in averaging 254 yards a game passing, but left in the third quarter with a possible shoulder separation after completing 9 of 21 for 131 yards.

"This is embarrassing to us, embarrassing to us as a university and to the state of Texas," said linebacker Brian Gamble. "We're going to do everything in our power not to let it happen again."

Oklahoma packed a game's worth of offense in the first half, then polished it off with a 22-yard and 26-yard TD receptions by Smith and Daniels in the third quarter and a 27-yard field goal by Tim Duncan in the fourth. Duncan now is seven for seven on field goals and 30 of 30 on extra points.

The Sooners scored four touchdowns and kicked two field goals on their first six possessions of the game. They weren't stopped until an interception — a Heupel pass bounced off his receiver's chest — with 23 seconds left in the half.

OU scored on touchdown drives of 40, 71, 83 and 77 yards, and drove 75 and 16 yards to field goals.

The Sooners ran 60 offensive plays in the first half and gained 376 total yards — 103 on the ground and 273 through the air. Heupel hit 25 of 40 first-half passes for the 273 yards.

TEXAS A&M	0	6	0	0	—	6
OKLAHOMA	17	17	14	3	—	51

BUFFS MAKE AN ALTITUDE ADJUSTMENT, RIP OU

By Mac Bentley
The Daily Oklahoman, Oct. 30, 1999

BOULDER, COLO. — Feeling the effects of dizzying heights once again, Oklahoma tried to hang on.

It was a desperate situation all around for the 24th-ranked Sooners this afternoon, much of it their own making, as unranked, without-a-vote Colorado kept them swaying on their heels throughout a 38-24 victory before 48,194 fans at Folsom Field.

The setting for this game, the foothills of the Rocky Mountains, was nothing compared to the high Oklahoma was on after last week's 51-6 victory over Texas A&M, and their second visit to the national rankings this season will again be only a one-week stay.

The Buffaloes, the first team to play a nine-game stretch against Oklahoma without losing (8-0-1), had the Sooners searching for ways to keep quarterback Josh Heupel safe from blitzes; to get some rhythm in the offense; to find a way to stop the Buffaloes; and to keep from committing penalties that had not been a problem most of this season.

Oklahoma, desperate enough to attempt five second-half fourth-down plays needing 8, 8, 9, 10 and 10 yards, didn't completely solve any of those dilemmas and fell to 4-3 on the season and 2-2 in the Big 12 South.

OU needs two victories in its final four games against Missouri, Iowa State, Oklahoma State and Texas Tech, a prospect that looked much brighter after last week's thumping of Texas A&M.

Heupel, who hit just 26 of 58 passes, basically had very little chance against the Buffaloes' blitzing. His was often a desperate situation as he threw numerous poor passes under extreme pressure, or while being hit, or before his receivers were ready, or when they took a different route than he expected.

Heupel threw four interceptions and three more came awfully close. He fumbled the ball at the OU 10, with Reggie Skinner saving the possession for a punt. Skinner later fumbled at the CU 2, with Stockar McDougle recovering, and OU scored on the next play.

"The plan was to have a number of blitzes ready and whichever one sorted itself out as the best was the one we would try to stay with," Colorado coach Gary Barnett said. "I don't think they ever stopped that (safety blitz). We had it pretty much all day

"We hit the quarterback and that's what we wanted to do."

The penalties were a mix of mental errors. Heupel got one himself for his snap count, OU got a delay of game coming out of a time-out, twice they had holding penalties that offset what would have been critical CU penalties, they had more than 11 men on the field on more than one occasion and an illegal receiver downfield nullified a Jeff Ferguson-to-Chris Hammons conversion of a fake punt on fourth-and-eight from the CU 45 with four minutes left in the third period.

"Mentally we were terrible," OU coach Bob Stoops said. "We made way too many penalties, we threw an interception on a screen pass ... we just didn't give ourselves much chance to win, on either side of the ball."

Oklahoma, losing 30 yards on three quarterback sacks, finished with minus-11 yards rushing on 17 attempts. None of the Sooners' 17 first downs came by rushing, and that's the first time Colorado has done that to a team since doing so to Nebraska in 1961.

Defensively, Oklahoma gave up 537 yards, 166 of that coming on five touchdown plays. Moschetti hit 22 of 31 attempts for 382 yards, including 49- and 88-yard TD passes to Javon Green.

In the fourth quarter, Heupel hit Reggie Skinner on a 6-yard shovel pass to pull the Sooners to within 24-17, but CU scored less than four minutes later on a 14-yard TD pass to Daniel Graham.

OU would again score on a 49-yard pass to Jarrail Jackson, but Colorado answered back less than a minute later when Green, taking advantage of a fallen Pee Wee Woods, took a pass in the wide open and sailed down the sideline for an 88-yard scoring play with 8:37 left.

Desperate? OU went for it on fourth-and-8 from the CU 12 less than a minute into the fourth quarter. The TD pass to Jackson was on a fourth-and-9 play from the CU 49 with 8:37 remaining. The Sooners failed on two fourth-and-10 plays in the final seven minutes.

OKLAHOMA	3	7	0	14	—	24
COLORADO	7	7	10	14	—	38

DEFENSE REGISTERS SHUTOUT AS SOONERS TAME TIGERS

By Mac Bentley
The Daily Oklahoman, Nov. 6, 1999

N ORMAN — There's no place like home, there's no place like home, there's no place ... well, you get the idea.

Oklahoma was clicking its heels over another Owen Field victory today, its fourth of the season and fourth by a wide margin. The convincing, methodical, 37-0 thumping of Missouri, though, leaves the Sooners facing a familiar challenge:

Can they take this act on the road?

They've already had four chances, but the three losses in this five-victory season have all come away from Memorial Stadium and the one road win, at Louisville, had to be pulled out in the fourth quarter after the Cardinals pushed them to a 21-21 tie after three.

"For whatever reasons, we've been very fortunate to come out and play well," Stoops said of OU's home-field experience. "The crowd's been behind us; it's always a great atmosphere, another perfect day to play."

Indeed. The biggest crowd of a sold-out season, 74,966, was

treated to sunshine, temperatures around 80 degrees and the Sooners' second shutout of the season. Until the 49-0 victory over Indiana State in the opener, OU hadn't posted a shutout since 1993, and now the Sooners have two in a season for the first time since 1987.

The Sooners, 3-2 in the Big 12, have outscored four opponents at home 178-16.

"That's great. Hopefully we can do something on the road," Stoops said. "You've got to be able to win on the road as well as home if you're going to be a team that's a factor in the conference."

The Sooners likely will be reminded of last week's disappointing performance at Colorado, coming off their best game of the year, as they pack their bags for next week's road trip to Iowa State. But they won't worry about that until Monday.

"Felt good to go out and execute in all parts of the game pretty well today," Stoops said. "Fairly solid all the way through. But I'm sure we'll find some things come Monday that we can get on them about.

"Our players came in the locker room, nobody's too happy about anything, everyone realizes it was a good solid win and we're going to keep pushing through the end of the year to continue to build and get better."

The Sooners led 10-0 at the half after letting some scoring opportunities slip through their fingers, then got a spark from punt return ace Jarrail Jackson early in the second half.

First Jackson returned a punt 42 yards to the Missouri 24-yard line, setting up a three-play TD drive. Seth Littrell scored from the 8, and it was 17-0 less than three minutes into the third quarter.

OU then got an interception by linebacker Roger Steffen on a ball deflected by Roy Williams and/or Torrence Marshall — even they weren't sure — and returned to the Mizzou 11. Two plays later quarterback Josh Heupel hit Damien Mackey on an 11-yard slant for a 24-0 lead less than two minutes later.

Later, Jackson bolted 70 yards up the middle on another punt return, taking it all the way for a 30-0 lead less three minutes into the fourth quarter.

"It's something we've worked on extensively through the year, but really in the last three or four weeks emphasizing the return, and it's helping," said Stoops, whose club has gotten great returns on kickoffs but little production on punts. "Players are picking up some good blocks, and (Jackson) is doing a nice job getting it upfield.

"He really gave us good field position all day."

Jackson set a school record for punt returns with 146 yards.

The Sooner defense held Missouri to just 274 yards. Tiger quarterback Jim Dougherty hit 18 of 38 passes for 169 yards, didn't have a touchdown and was intercepted twice. He had 13 passes deflected by OU defenders and his longest completion was just 19 yards.

Missouri pulled freshman Justin Gage out of redshirt in the second half, but he went 0 for 3 and Dougherty was reinserted.

Missouri (4-5 and 1-5 in the Big 12) penetrated OU's 30-yard line three times in the first half and twice in the second, but was shut out for the second time in three weeks (Kansas, 21-0). The Tigers converted just three of 19 third-down attempts and were shutout on four fourth-down tries.

Besides Steffen, the walk-on starting his third game, OU got an interception by Williams in the first quarter that set up a 56-yard drive to a field goal.

Linebacker Rocky Calmus had OU's only sack, and his nine tackles were second only to safety Rodney Rideau's 12.

Stoops obviously was pleased with the defensive effort, but wants to see more.

"We've got to do it next week, and after that we've got to do it again," he said. "Today they played well, met the challenge, played aggressively and did the things you wanted them to do. Means nothing if they don't come out and do it again next week. That's their challenge."

MISSOURI	0	0	0	0	—	0
OKLAHOMA	10	0	14	13	—	37

SOONERS GAIN 301 YARDS ON GROUND, RIP CYCLONES

By Mac Bentley
The Daily Oklahoman, Nov. 13, 1999

AMES, IOWA — Dared to run, Oklahoma ran and ran and ran against Iowa State today.

Unlike any team they've faced in this season of the pass at OU, the Sooners were confronted with a run-or-else option by the Cyclones. They answered with their best rushing attack in nearly two seasons; their best since this program was still entertaining thoughts of a return to the wishbone.

The passing game wasn't working today, so the Sooners came up with 301 yards on the ground to whip Iowa State, 31-10, before 37,073 fans at Jack Trice Stadium.

Freshman Quentin Griffin picked up 123 yards on 11 carries before leaving with a bruised hip early in the third quarter. Reggie Skinner came on and picked up 116 yards, also in 11 carries.

It was the best day on the ground since last year's team picked up 310 yards in the season opener against North Texas.

"We just feel fortunate to come up here and have a strong second half to seal the victory," coach Bob Stoops said. "(I'm) probably the most proud of our offensive line and our backs, to be able to run the ball and use the clock in the second half and still get the yards."

Griffin averaged 11.2 yards per carry, Skinner 10.5, as the Sooners, who struggled offensively in the first half, unleashed a 315-yard, three-touchdown performance in the second.

Oklahoma is now 6-3, 4-2 in the Big 12, and bowl-eligible for the first time since a 6-6 season in 1994. It was OU's first victory on the road in the Big 12 this year, and their 12th straight win at Jack Trice Stadium since it opened in 1975.

Iowa State fell to 4-6, 1-6 in the Big 12, with its fourth straight loss.

"All the games we've played well we've run well," Stoops said. "Over a hundred in all of them."

But this is the first time OU pretty much had to run the ball to win. Even in the five previous victories when the Sooners have had more than 100 yards on the ground, that wasn't half what they got through the air.

This time, the running game had a 301-180 advantage.

Why run? Quarterback Josh Heupel was not having a good day and, to compound the situation, the Cyclones were dropping everyone into coverage all day.

"I'd say they dropped more than any team we've played, no question, and that's why the run was there so frequently," offensive coordinator Mike Leach said. "They blitzed a little bit, not very much. They dropped everybody in the secondary and for the most part wanted to stay on top of us."

Late in the third quarter, Heupel had hit 15 of 31 passes for 108 yards. The Sooners had squandered outstanding field position in the first quarter and were thanking their defense for the 17-3 lead at the half and 24-3 lead midway through the third period.

The OU defense held Darren Davis, the country's fifth-leading rusher, to a season-low 53 yards. It was the third straight game for Davis to get fewer than 100 yards. Texas held him to 67 two weeks ago and Texas Tech held him to 96 last week. He had rushed for at least 100 yards in his first seven games, more than 200 twice.

"That's hard to do," Stoops said. "I said coming in and still do believe he's as good as there is in the country. Some of the runs he had out there today, I just shook my head. It's amazing what he can do.

"It was a good, disciplined effort on our defense's part to stay gap sound and to tackle well most of the day."

OU could have put the game away early but couldn't take full advantage of some outstanding field position. The Sooners first five possessions started at their own 41, the ISU 21, their own 35, the ISU 38 and their own 38.

They settled for a field goal and a touchdown, not getting a first down until their fourth possession. They put together a 72-yard drive in the second quarter, thanks in large part to runs of 16 and 27 yards by Griffin, the latter for the score and a 17-0 lead.

Griffin would dash 44 yards to an apparent TD in the third quarter, but a holding penalty shortened it to a 42-yard gain, set the Sooners back to the ISU 12 and they scored two plays later on a Seth Littrell run from the 3. Griffin was done for the day.

OU scored late in the game on a 26-yard pass to Josh Norman, but it was the only pass play on a 92-yard drive.

"Offensively, I thought we had a shaky first half, really from top to bottom, outside of Quentin Griffin," Leach said. "I thought in the second half we played real well. I thought everybody played well. I think that's a pretty good effort by everybody."

The 302 yards rushing marks the second-best effort against the Cyclones this season. Only Nebraska, in a 49-14 victory at Lincoln, rushed for more (439).

"It's good to be able to do both," Stoops said of the passing and running. "We've always said we've wanted to do both. We're getting better, we're growing in it."

OKLAHOMA	10	7	7	7 —	31
IOWA STATE	0	3	0	7 —	10

RAIDERS STUN SOONERS, CONVOLUTE BOWL PICTURE

By Mac Bentley
The Daily Oklahoman, Nov. 20, 1999

LUBBOCK, TEX. — Slow down that bowl express.

Texas Tech muddied the waters for Oklahoma's postseason, and the Big 12's as well today, with an impressive 38-28 victory over the Sooners.

The Red Raiders added themselves to the bowl pool, finishing the regular season with a 6-5 record, and made the Sooner finale with Oklahoma State next week all the more important.

It makes it a must-win game for the 6-4 Sooners, who could wind up as one of four Big 12 teams with a 6-5 record and one of eight bowl-eligible teams in a conference that has six, perhaps seven, bowl opportunities.

The Sooners are always an attractive bowl possibility because of their tradition and following, but without a victory against Oklahoma State they will have finished the season with two straight losses and will be 0-3 against the other teams — Colorado, Tech and OSU — with a 6-5 record.

It could have been different in today's game, played before 42,020 fans at Jones Stadium and in sunshine and 60-degree temperatures.

The Sooners overcame a 10-0 deficit to take a 21-10 lead before halftime and had an opportunity to build on that lead in the final minute of the half, but the only interception of the game was turned into a Texas Tech field goal.

The Red Raiders, finishing 5-3 in the Big 12, went on to score the game's next 25 points to send Coach Spike Dykes off on a happy note. Dykes announced his resignation following the game.

"That was a big factor," Sooner coach Bob Stoops said of the interception, which was caused by a miscommunication between quarterback Josh Heupel and receiver Brandon Daniels. "Instead of 21-10 with a chance to build on the lead, hopefully maybe discourage them some, but it gives them life and gets them right back into it.

"You can't turn the ball over. You can't do that anywhere and win. It's been the same scenario every game we've lost on the road. Turned the ball over a bunch and don't get many ourselves on defense, and there you have it."

The Sooners, 4-3 in the Big 12, finished with 401 total yards to 359 for Texas Tech. Through three quarters, OU had a 17-8 advantage in first downs over the Raiders but trailed, 31-21. Chalk that up to big plays made by Tech, which was playing with a redshirt freshman quarterback, Kliff Kingsbury, making his first start because of injury to Rob Peters.

■ On Tech's second play of the day, tailback Sam Morris streaked down the middle for a 32-yard touchdown reception.

■ On the first play of the next possession, the Raiders ran a flea-flicker netting 75 yards on a pass from Kingsbury to tight end Tim Winn. It carried to the 4, and OU held Tech to a field goal and 10-0 lead.

■ After the interception, which occurred with 35 seconds left in the first half, Tech set up at its own 42 and immediately connected on a 28-yard pass to Morris, setting up a field goal that narrowed OU's lead to 21-13.

■ In the third quarter, after Tech had pulled within 21-16, Kyle Shipley knocked the ball loose from an almost-passing Heupel, and it was kicked around before Kevin Curtis finally picked it up at the 8 and dived to the OU 1. The Raiders scored in two plays, converted a 2-pointer and had the lead for good at 24-21.

■ The killer came later in the third quarter as Tech set up at its own 33 following a punt. Kingsbury ran a bootleg and was almost sacked by Bary Holleyman, but escaped and eluded another defender before spotting Morris all alone downfield. It went for a 67-yard TD and a 31-21 lead with 1:13 left in the third quarter.

"Those are pretty elementary things. You've got to stay deep on a scramble and not let people get behind you," Sooner defensive coordinator Mike Stoops said. "It's a lack of execution, a lack of discipline and it's a lack of intensity. We weren't ready to play like we did the last two weeks, and they were ready.

"They whipped us pretty good."

The real whipping may have come in the fourth quarter.

The first lasted 5:40 before stalling at the OU 34 and the second lasting four minutes and one second before ending with an 18-yard TD pass and a 38-21 lead with 3:54 remaining.

By then, OU's fourth-quarter offense amounted to six plays, netting 13 yards and a punt.

"They ran the ball in the fourth quarter, mushed it at us," Bob Stoops said. OU drove 80, 65 and 77 yards for its three first-half touchdowns.

Heupel hit Daniels for a 29-yard gain on a deep crossing route to key the first drive, got the second touchdown on a 44-yard pass to Damien Mackey and then hit Jarrail Jackson on a 42-yard gain to set up a 13-yard run for the third touchdown by Quentin Griffin.

OKLAHOMA	14	7	0	7	—	28
TEXAS TECH	10	3	18	7	—	38

———— OU ————

SOONERS BLOW OUT POKES, FINISH 5-0 AT HOME

By John Rohde
The Daily Oklahoman, Nov. 27, 1999

NORMAN — Bedlam aside, Oklahoma treated Oklahoma State no differently than any other football team on Owen Field this season.

The largest home crowd of the decade (75,374) watched the Sooners cap a 5-0 home record with a 44-7 disposal of the Cowboys today. It gives OU its first undefeated season at home since 1987.

Afterward, security guards thwarted a half-hearted attempt from a couple of dozen fans to tear down both goal posts.

The outcome snapped the Sooners' two-game losing streak against OSU in Norman, where the Cowboys hadn't lost since a 31-0 whitewash in 1993 when they managed just one first down (by penalty).

OU outscored its opponents 222-23 at home this season.

Today's domination joined previous Norman conquests of Indiana State (49-0), Baylor (41-10), Texas A&M (51-6) and Missouri (37-0).

The Cowboys' lone score today came on an interception return. It was the first time this season the Oklahoma State offense did not score a point.

"If you think about it, this is our third shutout," OU coach Bob Stoops said.

With representatives from the Alamo and Independence bowls in attendance, the Sooners upped their overall record to 7-4, their best showing since qualifying for the Gator Bowl in 1993.

OU finishes in a three-way tie for second in the Big 12 South Division at 5-3.

Meanwhile, for the second straight year, the Cowboys finish 5-6 overall and 3-5 in the South while failing to become bowl eligible.

Bowl bids are not expected to be offered until after the Big 12 Championship game in San Antonio on Dec. 4, when the trickle-down effect commences due to the various conference tie-ins.

More than likely, the Sooners are bound for the Alamo Bowl (Dec. 28) in San Antonio against Penn State, the Insight.com Bowl (Dec. 31) in Tucson, Ariz., against Big East runner-up Miami or Boston College or the Independence Bowl against Mississippi (Dec. 31).

OSU was without four starters — tight end Marcellus Rivers, cornerback Alvin Porter, cornerback Evan Howell and strong safety J.B. Flowers — who were suspended for violation of team rules last weekend.

The Cowboys still utilized their tight ends with Bryan Blackwood and Khary Jackson combining for 99 yards on seven catches. That was the highlight of the offense, however.

OU junior quarterback Josh Heupel picked apart the depleted OSU secondary by completing 22 of 32 passes for 287 yards and two touchdowns while going to eight different receivers.

The Cowboys averaged just 3.2 yards per play. Their longest drive was 37 yards on their opening march that stalled at the OU 43. Their deepest penetration was the OU 18, which ended with a fumble.

OSU was 5-of-17 on third-down conversions and had to punt 10 times.

The Sooners' offense amassed 325 yards, its third-lowest output of the season.

"Defensively, for the most part, our guys kept us in the ball game, but that's been typical the whole year," OSU coach Bob Simmons said after losing for the first time on Owen Field. "On the other hand, our offense simply did not execute."

OU took a 7-0 lead with 4:24 left in the first quarter when Heupel completed a quick 3-yard pass in the flat to Brandon Daniels.

With 12:48 remaining in the second quarter and under heavy pressure, Heupel threw an interception to OSU linebacker Terrell Knauls, who returned it untouched 23 yards for a touchdown to tie the score.

OU responded with a 55-yard, 10-play drive capped by a 4-yard TD run from fullback Seth Littrell with 3:26 in the half.

After a halftime ceremony that honored OU's 1974 and 1975 national championship teams, the Sooners pushed the lead to 21-7 on the third play of the third quarter when Heupel found a streaking Curtis Fagen in the middle of the field for a 73-yard touchdown strike, the longest pass play against OSU this season.

OU sophomore place-kicker Tim Duncan converted a 31-yard field goal at the 12:21 mark of the fourth quarter on a drive that was set up by Corey Heinecke's interception of a Tony Lindsay pass.

With 6:06 left in the game, Heupel scored on a 7-yard bootleg after faking a handoff to offensive tackle Stockar McDougle, who played in the backfield for several plays during the fourth quarter.

OU cornerback Mike Woods pushed the Sooners' lead to 38-7 with a 43-yard interception return for a touchdown with 4:13 left.

J.T. Thatcher then slammed the door with an 81-yard punt return with 1:12 remaining, OU's longest punt return in five years.

OKLAHOMA STATE	0	7	0	0 —	7
OKLAHOMA	7	7	7	23 —	44

OU

BINKLEY BOOTS 39-YARD FIELD GOAL TO DEFEAT OU

By Mac Bentley
The Daily Oklahoman, Dec. 31, 1999

S HREVEPORT, LA. — The 20th century and Oklahoma's first football season under Bob Stoops ended within an hour of each other tonight.

Neither was too shabby. Both, it could be said, offered promise of better days.

The Sooners rallied from their biggest deficit of the season to take the lead with 2:17 left in the 24th Independence Bowl. But Mississippi pulled the rug out with a field goal as time ran out for a 27-25 victory.

It was a 39-yard field goal by Les Binkley that the Sooners will remember as they head into the 21st century. OU scored three second-half touchdowns, the third one with 2:17 left in the game, to take a 25-24 lead.

But a 42-yard kickoff runback by Deuce McAllister sparked the Rebels to the game-winning drive.

The victory gave Ole Miss an 8-4 record. Oklahoma closes its first season under Stoops at 7-5.

The Rebels picked up their fourth straight bowl victory, including a 35-18 win over Texas Tech in this same Independence Stadium last year.

The loss gives Oklahoma a 5-3-1 record in December bowl games, 20-12-1 in bowl games overall. It was their first post-season appearance since 1994.

Sooner quarterback Josh Heupel threw three touchdown passes in the second half. He hit Jarrail Jackson for 3 yards and Brandon Daniels for 41 in the third quarter, then found freshman Quentin Griffin from 17 yards out for what looked like the winning touchdown with 2:17 left in the game.

Setting up at their own 43 after McAllister's runback, the Rebels moved 30 yards on four plays and an OU penalty (12 men on the field), then picked up 5 yards on two running plays to the OU 22-yard line. The Rebels then let the clock run down to three seconds before calling time-out and asking Binkley to win the game.

The field goal was the 16th in 18 attempts for Binkley this season, his 11th success in 12 tries inside 40 yards.

It was a record-setting night for Heupel, who was voted the game'soutstanding offensive player. He hit 39 of 54 passes for 390 yards, establishing Oklahoma bowl records and Independence Bowl records.

Mississippi cornerback Tim Strickland, who intercepted a pass in the end zone and also caused a fumbled, was voted the defensive player of the game.

The Sooners had their chances but turned the ball over four times, missed a 35-yard field goal and failed on two fourth-down plays — a fake punt and a fake field goal.

"We made a few too many mistakes that cost us the game," coach Bob Stoops said. "That's the way it goes, but a well-fought game and I couldn't be more proud of our players to come back the second half and take the lead.

"The bottom line is you can't turn the football over. You count all the points we lost on turnovers in the red zone, and we win."

It was the closest game of the season for OU, which lost by four points at Notre Dame but really didn't challenge at the end.

"I felt like we deserved one for what we've been through in the fourth quarter, particularly at the end of the season," said Mississippi coach David Cutcliffe, whose club lost it's final two regular-season games by three points each.

The Sooners trailed by 18 at the half, 21-3, their largest deficit of the season.

Oklahoma cut the lead on its first possession of the third quarter, driving 73 yards on nine plays and getting a touchdown on the 3-yarder by Jackson. A 21-yard end-around by Brandon Daniels was the big play, carrying the Sooners to the Mississippi 15-yard line.

The Sooners came back later in the period to drive 80 yards on six plays and pull within 21-18.

All six plays were Heupel completions, with the payoff being the 41-yarder to Daniels.

Ole Miss then put together a 14-play, 70-yard, seven-minute drive that resulted in a 29-yard field goal by Binkley and a 24-18 Mississippi lead four minutes into the fourth quarter.

OU came right back, driving 45 yards to the Ole Miss 19-yard line, but Heupel was sacked and fumbled with Anthony Sims recovering for the Rebels at the 20-yard line.

OU's defense held, and the Sooners got the ball back on a punt at their own 21-yard line with 4:15 left in the game. They drove 79 yards in six plays and two minutes, with the TD again coming off a Heupel scramble — a 17-yard completion to Griffin.

"He said my man wasn't hanging on me so run a wheel route down the field, and Josh saw me," Griffin said.

Ole Miss held a 270-213 advantage in total yards at the half, including 158 through the air on 12-of-18 passing by Romaro Miller, despite two interceptions. Heupel hit 21 of 33 in the first 30 minutes for 184 yards, with one interception.

The first quarter saw four turnovers — two Mississippi interceptions and two OU fumbles.

Oklahoma had a good drive on its first possession, moving 37 yards on a 12-yard run by Griffin, an 11-yard pass to Jackson and a 14-yard pass to Daniels, but three incompletions led to a 35-yard field-goal attempt and Tim Duncan missed wide left.

Mississippi responded with a quick, four-play drive to the game's first touchdown. The score came on a 25-yard pass to McAllister, who wasn't picked up coming out of the backfield. It was set up on a 45-yard completion from Miller to Maurice Flournoy, who beat OU defender Mike Woods down the left sideline.

OLE MISS	7	14	0	6	—	27
OKLAHOMA	3	0	15	7	—	25

THE
2000 SEASON

MANSHIP STEALS SHOW AS OU RIPS UTEP

By George Schroeder
The Daily Oklahoman, Sept. 2, 2000

NORMAN — Perhaps this is a measure of how far the Oklahoma Sooners have come in a year.

They won big tonight, beating Texas-El Paso, 55-14, as 74,761 watched at Memorial Stadium.

And left feeling unsatisfied.

"We know we didn't play up to OU ball," sophomore strong safety Roy Williams said.

Said OU coach Bob Stoops: "We can be very critical, and we still won, 55-14. Everyone was wondering why we had so many miscues. And that's good."

It took freshman tailback Renaldo Works to inject life into an otherwise drowsy opener. Works scored three fourth-quarter touchdowns to stretch the margin from comfortable toward luxurious.

"Renaldo stole the show," Stoops said.

Works reignited the crowd — and the Sooners.

The largest crowd for a season opener since 1988 endured the hottest season opener in school history. It was 106 degrees at kickoff. And it might have been more than the heat that lulled many of the fans into a stupor for three quarters.

OU led, 34-14, entering the fourth quarter, but a plethora of mistakes had derailed opportunities to widen the margin.

"We didn't feel good at all," Stoops said.

OU was the recipient of seven UTEP turnovers, but failed to capitalize on many.

For the most part, the defense played solidly, scoring one touchdown — on Williams' 35-yard, second-quarter interception return — and setting up five more scores by snatching UTEP turnovers.

That helped mask an uneven night for the offense and the defense, which at times allowed UTEP to move the football. OU was penalized nine times for 70 yards.

"We were far too sloppy for us to be the kind of team we want to be the rest of the year," Stoops said. "Far too many mistakes."

OU led, 27-7, at halftime and needed only 28 third-quarter seconds to push the lead to 34-7 — J.T. Thatcher's interception led to a 21-yard touchdown pass from Josh Heupel to Antwone Savage.

But the Sooners seemed to doze off until Works emerged in the final quarter. Works finished with 98 yards on 19 carries and scored on runs of 19, 6 and 5 yards.

Until the freshman from Tulsa Washington emerged late, the game's dominant theme was of unease for the Sooners.

For much of the night, OU's offense clunked along like a jalopy running on bad gas.

Heupel completed 18 of 36 passes for 274 yards, with two touchdowns and one interception. But he was 12-of-25 at halftime, and endured a stretch of seven straight incompletions in the second quarter.

"The whole offense was off-rhythm in the second quarter," Stoops said.

The running game, a point of emphasis in the off-season, sputtered until Works' late work. And other big plays went against OU — including an apparent 57-yard touchdown pass from Heupel to Damian Mackey that was waved off when Mackey was flagged for offensive pass interference.

Earlier, Mackey fumbled away a 42-yard reception — and UTEP

took advantage to tie the game at 7-7.

There were plenty of mistakes to go around.

The Sooners played without starting middle linebacker Torrance Marshall and reserve free safety Brandoon Everage. Both players were suspended for what Stoops called "unspecified reasons."

Stoops said they "should be back this week."

There were highlights:

■ Junior defensive end Cory Heinecke pounced on a fumble at the UTEP 17 to set up OU's first touchdown, and later caused another fumble.

■ Sophomore tailback Quentin Griffin raced 36 yards with an improvised pass from Heupel to set up the Sooners' second score.

■ And there was Works' work.

In the fourth quarter, the 6-foot-1, 208-pounder rambled 39 yards in two plays — 20, then 19 yards for a touchdown — to make it 41-14.

After junior linebacker Rocky Calmus returned a fumble to the 12, Works needed two plays — dragging defenders much of the way — for another score.

Works finished things with a 5-yard touchdown run.

Works carried 15 times for 79 yards in the fourth quarter.

"If it's there, we'll keep going to it," Stoops said.

UTEP	7	0	7	0	—	14
OKLAHOMA	17	10	7	21	—	55

SOONERS TAKE THE EASY ROUT AGAINST ARKANSAS STATE

By George Schroeder
The Daily Oklahoman, Sept. 9, 2000

NORMAN — This much we know.

In two games, the Oklahoma Sooners haven't been much tested.

As 74,730 fans watched tonight at Memorial Stadium, 20th-ranked OU opened with 28 straight points and rolled to a 45-7 victory over outmanned Arkansas State.

It was never competitive. The decisive moment might have come 18 months ago, when Arkansas State begged OU to push the game from last season's schedule to 2000.

If you're looking for a key moment from game day, try the coin toss. Arkansas State won, then deferred the decision to the second half — when it didn't matter.

The Sooners took the opening kickoff, marched 80 yards in 15 plays and were on their way to their second rout in as many games.

"A lot of good points in the game," said OU coach Bob Stoops, who celebrated his 40th birthday today. "Running, throwing, all of it, really. We were sharper than a week ago."

The second designated victim went down easier than the first. OU worked out several kinks that had bugged the Sooners in last week's 55-14 win over Texas-El Paso.

"Let's face it," Arkansas State coach Joe Hollis said. "OU didn't schedule Arkansas State to lose … . I think they'll be tested when they play against a better football team."

Arkansas State wasn't that team.

The Sooners amassed 533 total yards, including 208 rushing.

For the second time in school history, OU had a 300-yard passer, a 100-yard rusher and a 100-yard receiver in the same game. Those honors went to quarterback Josh Heupel (24 of 32 passes for 302 yards and three touchdowns), freshman tailback Renaldo Works (12 carries, 109 yards — including a 75-yard touchdown scamper) and sophomore receiver Andre Woolfolk (five catches, 102 yards and two touchdowns), respectively.

"No doubt, we feel better about ourselves this week than we did last week," Heupel said. "We had much more rhythm in our offense."

The Sooners punted just once and were stopped only by themselves. Eleven penalties for 95 yards derailed what could have been a really, really big offensive performance. The flags and two missed field goals by Tim Duncan were the only glaring flaws.

OU held Arkansas State to 275 yards, including just 84 on the ground. In a 38-31, double-overtime loss last week at North Carolina State, the Indians had 181 rushing yards.

"That was our major emphasis, limiting the run," Stoops said. "Overall, we had a really solid (defensive) effort."

"Josh was very sharp," Stoops said. "He found open people and delivered the football. And our guys caught the football better today."

With three touchdown passes, Heupel carved another notch in OU's record books. The third touchdown pass, a 35-yard strike to Woolfolk early in the third quarter, pushed OU ahead, 35-7, and gave Heupel 35 career TD passes, tying him with Cale Gundy atop the school rankings.

Most of the damage was done in the first half, when OU scored four touchdowns before Arkansas State crossed midfield.

The eventual outcome was evident after the opening possession, when the Sooners moved 80 yards in 15 crisp plays. Heupel
completed 4 of 6 passes for 41 yards. The other 39 yards came on the
ground, including Heupel's 1-yard sneak for the touchdown.

Later in the first quarter, Thatcher jump-started his career
performance, returning Andy Shatley's punt 66 yards for a score.
Thatcher grabbed the line drive, darted up the middle, then veered
right and raced untouched for the touchdown.

After Thatcher's second consecutive big return — a 30-yarder —
OU needed six plays to stretch the lead to 21-0. Heupel connected
with Mackey for a 21-0 lead with 14:55 left in the first half.

OU led, 28-0, after Heupel hit Woolfolk for a 19-yard score
midway through the second quarter.

The second half had the flavor of a scrimmage. After Heupel and
Woolfolk connected to make it 35-7 early in the third quarter,
nothing much happened until Works' big run. He turned a routine
toss sweep into another highlight, turning the corner, racing down
the sideline and then cutting across field for the score.

"If he stays straight ahead, he's tackled after a 30-yard gain,"
Stoops said.

ARKANSAS ST.	0	7	0	0	—	7
OKLAHOMA	14	14	7	10	—	45

SOONERS BLOW OUT RICE IN SECOND HALF

By George Schroeder
The Daily Oklahoman, Sept. 23, 2000

NORMAN — Brian Bosworth gave the Oklahoma Sooners a pregame pep talk today.

At halftime, senior center Bubba Burcham grasped the Boz's meaning.

The legendary former linebacker, at Owen Field for a reunion of the 1985 national championship team, told the current Sooners they "can't just expect tradition to happen," Burcham said.

"He said we have to make our own tradition," Burcham said. "We have to make things happen."

After a while, the Sooners did.

The final score — Oklahoma 42, Rice 14 — shows another rout. In the final moments, the starters relaxed on the sidelines. And many of the fans — attendance was announced as 74,794, but there were some empty seats — got a head start on the drive home.

But for almost three quarters, this wasn't a romp. Helped by three OU turnovers, Rice (1-3) gave the 16th-ranked Sooners all they wanted before wearing out.

OU led, 21-6, at halftime. But several players said the margin —

and its method — were unsatisfying. And Burcham reflected on Bosworth's message.

"We got out there and we were just expecting things to happen because of who we are," Burcham said of OU's first-half performance. "That kind of hit me at halftime. We have to go out and attack guys and make things happen."

The Sooners didn't tuck their third win away until late in the third quarter. Keyed by Quentin Griffin's pinball running, OU scored two touchdowns in a 2:58 span and another in the fourth.

"I guess a good, frustrating, 42-14 win," coach Bob Stoops said.

But Stoops said the trouble was the turnovers, not motivation.

"I thought we were fine. I don't think you need to come out and tear down the stadium to be ready to play," Stoops said. "They're mature, smart kids. They know what it takes to win."

However it happened, OU is 3-0 — "beats the heck out of 0-3 or 2-1," Stoops said. The Sooners won all their non-conference games for the first time since 1993, and outscored their opponents 142-35.

There were plenty of positives. OU piled up 532 yards. Heupel threw for 324 yards and, with a 4-yard pass to Josh Norman in the third quarter, became OU's all-time leader with 36 touchdown passes. But he threw two interceptions.

Griffin, who had been overshadowed by freshman Renaldo Works in the first two games, rushed for 117 yards and three TD's on just 14 carries. The effort included plenty of broken tackles.

Rice, which entered the game averaging 232 yards rushing, managed 145. Led by linebackers Rocky Calmus (14 tackles) and Torrance Marshall (11 tackles), OU stopped the fullback and stuffed Rice for the most part.

"That type of offense is aggravating," Stoops said. "You just get caught up supporting the run and they have a tendency to sneak somebody by you.

"But we were really pretty solid most of the day."

OU's offense aggravated Stoops at times, as well — especially the first half, when it had two turnovers.

To achieve its halftime lead, OU had to stop a fourth-down conversion try by Rice, then convert a fourth-down gamble of its own.

Trailing 14-6 midway through the second quarter, Rice faced fourth-and-inches at the OU 13, but fullback Jamie Tyler was stuffed by tackle Cory Heinecke. Later in the quarter, OU faced fourth-and-3 at the Rice 34.

"I just felt at that point we needed something to happen," Stoops said. "It was worth the gamble."

Heupel hit his roommate, Josh Norman, on a quick slant for 29 yards.

"That was a huge play," Heupel said, "to get momentum on our side." Three plays later, Heupel's sneak gave OU a 21-6 lead.

Stoops said the Sooners take a "business-like" approach to game preparation. He said halftime was the same: no screaming, just a few adjustments.

But a promising drive to start the third quarter ended when Heupel threw what he called an ill-advised pass that was tipped, then intercepted at the Rice 25.

Instead, Rice rolled 75 yards, keyed by quarterback Ben Wulf's 41-yard pass after a fake handoff. Corey Evans — Rice's other quarterback in what at times was an almost-every-play rotation — scored from 4 yards on an option keeper. A two-point conversion pulled Rice to within 21-14 with 7:47 left in the third quarter.

"We had hope," Rice coach Ken Hatfield said.

But OU took control with its running game. After realizing the Owls had begun dropping an extra defender into pass coverage, the Sooners moved 80 yards in seven plays — six runs — and 1:47.

Griffin's 21-yard run with 3:13 left pushed the lead back to two touchdowns. OU added two more touchdowns for the comfortable finish.

RICE	6	0	8	0	—	14
OKLAHOMA	14	7	14	7	—	42

SOONERS FORCE 7 TURNOVERS AGAINST KU

By George Schroeder
The Daily Oklahoman, Sept. 30, 2000

Norman — There wasn't a sigh of relief. Not exactly.

But when Andre Woolfolk gathered in Josh Heupel's perfectly feathered lob for a third-quarter touchdown, the Oklahoma Sooners certainly exhaled.

Don't be fooled by the final score. OU beat Kansas, 34-16, this afternoon. But as 74,811 fans watched at Memorial Stadium, the third-quarter touchdown gave the Sooners enough breathing room to put away the scrappy Jayhawks.

"We needed this game today," Heupel said. "We needed some tough times just to react and prepare for the rest of the conference season."

The Sooners' offense "sputtered," said offensive coordinator Mark Mangino. And the defense was truly a big-play unit: The Sooners made big plays and gave up some, too.

But OU is 4-0 for the first time since 1993.

The 14th-ranked Sooners laid to rest Kansas' three-game winning streak in the series. More important, OU is 1-0 in Big 12 play heading into the Texas game, which becomes an early South Division showdown.

Kansas (2-2, 0-1 in the Big 12) lost its 14th consecutive Big 12 road game, buried under seven turnovers, including five interceptions — are both school records.

"Turnovers were our demise," Kansas coach Terry Allen said.

Despite the turnovers, OU's victory came only after what Allen called a "ping-pong first half" that featured deep passes, open Kansas receivers and turnovers. It also featured the first lead by an OU opponent this season.

But OU took an eight-point lead into halftime, then grabbed control in the second half.

"It was almost like two different football games for us, the first half and second half," OU coach Bob Stoops said. "I'm glad some of the things happened."

The Sooners scored 10 points in the third quarter — more than enough cushion for the defense, which clamped down on the Jayhawks in the second half.

Kansas quarterback Dylen Smith had thrown for a career-high 216 yards by halftime. He frustrated OU defenders with his mobility, and torched several defensive backs with his strong, if not accurate, arm.

In the second half, Smith managed 42 yards. He was intercepted twice — bringing his game total to five picks — and sacked five times.

Counting a first-half sack, the Sooners nearly matched their season production of seven sacks. Kansas hadn't allowed a sack in its first three games.

"It was almost like we matured in the 20 minutes of halftime," Stoops said. "We covered better and the guys did a better job of closing on and tackling Smith, as well."

Kansas entered the game with the nation's top pass defense, allowing an average of 84 yards. Heupel completed 29 of 43 passes for 346 yards and a touchdown, with no interceptions.

"An excellent day," Stoops said.

Despite those numbers, the Sooners never found a rhythm, and resorted to trickery for the first time this season — out came the

Ninja formation — and Antwone Savage's 40-yard scamper on a reverse gave OU a 24-16 halftime lead.

"We couldn't establish consistency," Mangino said.

The Sooners could easily have been staring at a two-touchdown deficit in the first half.

Smith started things with an interception that led to an OU field goal. But his next pass was a 77-yard connection with Roger Ross that gave the Jayhawks an early 6-3 lead.

Kansas led, 16-10, in the second quarter when OU tight end Trent Smith's fumble gave Kansas possession deep in OU territory. But a moment later, Ramon Richardson stripped the football from Smith and Corey Callens recovered the fumble.

"A huge play," Heupel said.

The Sooners offense rolled 82 yards in eight plays to take the lead on Quentin Griffin's 13-yard run.

Then, after Brandon Everage's acrobatic interception, Savage raced untouched — helped by a block from Heupel — into the end zone.

"I told our players, 'Listen, we can play a lot better than we played in the first half,' said Stoops. 'We've done a lot of foolish things and we're still up eight points,'" he said.

The Heupel-to-Woolfolk connection with 3:59 left in the third quarter finally ended most of the suspense.

"That put a lot of pressure on them," Heupel said.

Moments earlier, Tim Duncan's 39-yard field goal stretched OU's lead to 11 points, 27-16. Heupel opened the Sooners' next possession with a 39-yard strike to Josh Norman.

Two plays later, his 22-yard lob found Woolfolk for the touchdown.

Until then, the Jayhawks were one play away from a razor-thin margin. On Kansas' previous possession, Smith had just missed hitting another open receiver deep. His pass too long for Harrison Hill, who had gotten beyond cornerback Derrick Strait.

| KANSAS | 13 | 3 | 0 | 0 | — | 16 |
| OKLAHOMA | 10 | 14 | 10 | 10 | — | 34 |

GRIFFIN SCORES RECORD 6 TD'S AGAINST UT

By George Schroeder
The Daily Oklahoman, Oct. 7, 2000

DALLAS — Amid the postgame delirium in the Cotton Bowl this afternoon, Oklahoma senior offensive tackle Scott Kempenich paused briefly, looked up at the scoreboard, and contemplated the Sooners' accomplishment.

Oklahoma 63. Texas 14.

"Dang! What's up with that?" Kempenich asked.

But weird as it sounds, the Sooners said afterward the performance wasn't completely unexpected.

Quentin Griffin led the way with a school-record six rushing touchdowns as 10th-ranked OU routed No. 11 Texas. As another sellout crowd of 75,587 watched — at least until the second quarter, when Texas fans began melting away toward the state fair's midway — the Sooners rolled to a 42-0 lead, then cruised to a record-setting day.

And then shrugged.

"We were confident coming in," OU coach Bob Stoops said.

But by 49 points?

"They're a good football team. But we can be pretty explosive,"

Stoops said. "I'm not totally surprised. We can get things going sometimes, and our kids were ready for this game. They understood the importance of it."

The only big surprise, the Sooners said, might have been how good it felt. OU snapped a three-game losing streak in the series, winning for first time since 1996.

"That," junior linebacker Rocky Calmus said, "was more than what I expected."

The win, which sets up a showdown with No. 4 Kansas State, was every bit as impressive as its margin.

On a soggy field — a light rain fell for much of the game — OU (5-0, 2-0 in the Big 12) rolled to touchdowns on its first five possessions. Add a defensive score, and with 4:43 left in the first half, OU led, 42-0.

The only remaining suspense was the final margin.

"We wanted 70," sophomore receiver Curtis Fagan said. "It would be nice even to get to 80."

Instead, the Sooners settled for the most points they've scored in the 95-game history of the series, and the series' second-largest margin, behind only OU's 50-0 win in 1908.

Heck, it was the biggest whipping OU has put on any opponent since beating Arkansas State 61-0 in 1992, and the most points scored by the Sooners since a 73-3 squeaker over New Mexico State in 1989.

"It wasn't even a game," said Texas coach Mack Brown, who apologized to his university, its student body and Longhorns fans for what he called "as poor a performance as I've seen out of a football team I was responsible for."

And Brown, who said he deserved all the blame, had another thought.

"It's one you'll never forget your whole life," Brown said.

The Sooners made sure they won't.

Afterward, senior defensive tackle Ryan Fisher grabbed the Ruf-Neks' giant OU flag and led a charge toward midfield, where he planted the flag. Senior offensive lineman Al Baysinger hitched a triumphant ride in the Sooner Schooner.

And the Sooners gathered in one relaxed, celebrating mass for a team photograph, complete with the scoreboard in the background.

"A keepsake," Stoops said.

They'll want to keep the videotape, too.

OU piled up 534 yards — another record against Texas. That included 245 rushing yards, and a 275-yard passing day from Heupel, who watched the last few minutes from the sidelines as first Nate Hybl and then Patrick Fletcher ran the offense.

Meanwhile, OU's defense limited Texas to 154 total yards and minus-7 rushing yards. Take away lost yardage on four sacks, and the Longhorns' rushing total was only 23 yards.

"We flew around and struck people all over the field," co-defensive coordinator Brent Venables said.

OU scored on its first five possessions. Meanwhile, the Sooner defense held Texas to one first down and forced punts on five of UT's first six possessions.

The Longhorns' other possession was a direct contribution to the uneven scoreboard — Calmus returned an interception 41 yards for a touchdown and a 35-0 lead.

"All cylinders clicked," Calmus said. "Every part of the game."

After Texas ran three plays and punted away its first possession, the Sooners needed five plays to grab the lead. Josh Heupel's 29-yard pass to Andre Woolfolk pushed OU up, 7-0.

After another Texas punt, the Sooners rolled 77 yards for a 14-0 lead.

Another Texas punt. Another OU score. Griffin's 2-yard run gave OU a 21-0 lead just 36 seconds into the second quarter. But none of the Sooners were satisfied. And the Longhorns weren't especially concerned.

The situation was familiar to both teams. In 1999, OU jumped to a 17-0 lead, but eventually succumbed in a 38-28 Texas win.

Not today.

"I told the guys I thought they'd have a surge early, the momentum usually changes in this game and it didn't," Brown said. "They had the surge, and they kept it."

On the sidelines, OU coaches reminded players. Players reminded teammates: "Finish."

"We picked up the momentum," sophomore receiver Damian Mackey said. "Coaches told us to get it and don't ever let it go. Our coaches gave us a talk. Go out there and play four quarters of your best football.

"It paid off."

OKLAHOMA	14	28	14	7	—	63
TEXAS	0	7	0	7	—	14

HEUPEL CONQUERS NO. 2 KANSAS STATE

By George Schroeder
The Daily Oklahoman, Oct. 14, 2000

MANHATTAN, KAN. — Oklahoma fans on the field were chanting, "We're No. 1!" And at least one Kansas State fan didn't argue.

Quietly amid the post-game mob scene, he went from Sooner to Sooner, offering congratulations for OU's 41-31 victory. And for one more achievement on a gray Saturday afternoon.

"Welcome back," he said.

The fan was only stating the obvious. As a KSU Stadium-record crowd of 53,011 watched — most wearing purple, mostly silent as the game wore on — eighth-ranked Oklahoma rolled to a big lead, then held on to edge No. 2 Kansas State.

And with the victory, the Sooners announced their return to college football's elite.

"Now, I think the country understands. OU is here," sophomore receiver Damian Mackey said. "And we're going to be here to stay."

Led by senior quarterback Josh Heupel's 29-of-37, 374-yard performance, the Sooners struck first, grabbed a 38-14 third-quarter lead with several big plays, then weathered a furious rally to snap Kansas State's 25-game home winning streak.

Tim Duncan's 24-yard field goal with 3:27 left sealed the victory, though it was Corey Callens' fourth-down tackle of Kansas State quarterback Jonathan Beasley with 2:46 left that sent the first of several oranges bouncing onto the field.

Thrown by OU fans, the fruit was a reminder of the past — it once signified the Sooners' postseason destination was the Orange Bowl as the Big Eight champion — and a symbol of what is possible in the present.

In the Bowl Championship Series format, the Orange Bowl will decide this year's national championship. And after today, OU's possible participation doesn't seem so farfetched.

OU is 6-0 for the first time since 1987, and 3-0 in Big 12 play. The Sooners are almost certain to move into the top five when the polls come out today, setting up an even bigger showdown in two weeks, when top-ranked Nebraska visits Norman.

"I think everybody is starting to realize what we can do," senior defensive tackle Ryan Fisher said. "Definitely, this has probably opened Nebraska's eyes."

Try everyone's eyes, Ryan.

OU shredded the nation's top-rated defense for 385 yards. After 78 yards in losses including four sacks, the rushing total was 11 yards. But that didn't account for Heupel.

"Their strategy was to play nine guys in the box and stop the run," offensive coordinator Mark Mangino said. "Apparently, they forgot No. 14 was back there. You can stop the run against us. We'll beat you with the pass."

When it counted, OU's defense slowed Beasley and the quick, talented Wildcats. Kansas State finishhed with 355 total yards, but went almost 27 minutes between touchdowns in the second, third and fourth quarters.

And after the Wildcats had rallied within seven points with two quick touchdowns — a 69-yard catch-and-run by Quincy Morgan and a blocked punt two minutes later — the defense stiffened in the final moments.

"We had some major defensive stands when they had some momentum," coach Bob Stoops said. "If they get a first down or get some things rolling again, then we've got a chance to be in a tough bind."

J.T. Thatcher's 93-yard, first-quarter kickoff return set up a touchdown that gave OU a 10-7 lead it never relinquished. Later in the half, Roy Williams intercepted a Jonathan Beasley pass, setting up another score.

And in the third quarter came the Sooners' biggest play.

Facing third and 26 — from the OU 26, senior quarterback Josh Heupel dumped a short pass to Antwone Savage near the right sideline. Savage faked, bounced inside and away from four defenders, then sped up the sideline into the end zone.

"That play was unbelievable," wide receivers coach Steve Spurrier said. "That must have been six guys that missed him."

With 9:30 left in the third quarter, OU led, 38-14. KSU Stadium was silent except for several pockets of screaming Sooners fans.

But Kansas State wasn't finished. The Wildcats drove for a field goal to pull within three touchdowns. And then, scored twice in 2:08.

First, senior receiver Quincy Morgan did his best imitation of Savage, turning a short catch. into a 69-yard touchdown.

Then, after three OU lost 5 yards on three plays, Drew Thalmann blocked Jeff Ferguson's punt. Terence Newman scooped up the football and returned it for a touchdown, pulling Kansas State to within 38-31 with 10:31 left.

But the Sooners punched back. OU overcame an interception on a halfback pass coaches later said was a mistake. After the defense held, Duncan's field goal capped a 12-play, 47-yard drive that consumed an important 4:10.

And OU's defense stopped the Wildcats twice more, and the celebration began.

"The history of being able to win on the road is huge for any team," Spurrier said. "And that's a sign that we can go play about anywhere. That's what I think is the biggest thing for our guys, because we knew it would be hostile, we knew they'd be mad, we knew they were No. 2 in the country and they knew this is one of their bigger games of the year. We came in here and played really well."

OKLAHOMA	17	14	7	3	—	41
KANSAS STATE	7	7	3	14	—	31

SOONERS CONQUER NO. 1 NEBRASKA

By George Schroeder
The Daily Oklahoman, Oct. 28, 2000

NORMAN — As the final seconds melted off the clock, Bubba Burcham gripped the errant orange tightly in his left hand — and snapped the football with his right.

After that final snap, Burcham joined the raucous celebration that erupted this afternoon on Owen Field.

Third-ranked Oklahoma 31, No. 1 Nebraska 14.

Any questions?

Thirteen seasons since the Sooners last held college football's preeminent position, they have returned. When the various rankings are released today — AP, coaches and the all-important Bowl Championship Series — OU will be No. 1.

"It's still all a blur," said Burcham, the Sooners' senior center.

It was more than an hour after that final snap. The bruised orange, one of many hurled onto the field by fans in the final moments, was still in Burcham's hand. His head was still spinning at the Sooners' accomplishment.

"It's a great feeling to be sitting where we are today," Burcham said. "It's been a long time. It's good to see us back on top."

OU (7-0, 4-0 in the Big 12) beat Nebraska (7-1, 4-1 in the Big 12) despite spotting the Huskers a 14-0 first-quarter deficit. As 75,989 watched — the 10th-largest crowd in Memorial Stadium history — the Sooners dominated the last three quarters and beat the Huskers for the first time since 1990.

How about this for an October surprise? That rugged stretch — Texas, Kansas State and Nebraska — that was supposed to define OU's season?

Turns out, it was the perfect storm.

"All we heard about was winning October, winning those three games," said junior linebacker Rocky Calmus, who had 16 tackles to help the Sooners stop Nebraska's power rushing game. "No one thought we could get one.

"But we got all three."

Today was certainly the biggest hurdle.

And early, it looked as if the Huskers would roll. But the Sooners got big plays from offense, defense and special teams in scoring 31 straight points.

"We had everything going our way early on," Nebraska coach Frank Solich said. "But the test of a good football team is when your backs are to the wall like that and how you respond. (Oklahoma) responded very well."

Nebraska raced to 167 yards and two touchdowns on its first 11 plays.

But OU held Nebraska scoreless on its last 11 possessions. The Huskers managed 161 yards in their final 59 plays.

"It happened so quickly," said senior defensive tackle Jeremy Wilson-Guest of Nebraska's quick start, which featured a 39-yard touchdown pass by Eric Crouch, then a 37-yard touchdown run by the talented quarterback.

"It was like, 'Wow! We've got to buckle up,' " Wilson Guest said. "From then on, our defense went toe-to-toe with 'em. And we stuck 'em."

The Huskers entered the game with a 379.7-yard rushing average, the nation's best, but finished with 195 against OU.

Part of that was because the Huskers were forced to play catch-up.

Much of it was because of OU's defense.

"I don't know if you'll see a stronger defensive performance against them, to be able to stop their run game that way," coach Bob Stoops. "From the second quarter on, it was just exceptional."

OU's defense was especially dominant in the second quarter, when Nebraska ran 15 plays and managed 16 yards.

That's also when the Sooners got untracked offensively. OU exploded for 24 second-quarter points to take control.

Players and coaches say there was no real concern when the Sooners fell behind.

"No one panicked," Stoops said. "We just had to get settled in."

Josh Heupel completed 20 of 34 passes for 300 yards and a touchdown after a 5-for-11 start.

In the decisive second quarter, Heupel was 7 of 10 for 149 yards and a touchdown.

Heupel's 34-yard connection with Curtis Fagan pulled the Sooners into a 14-14 tie with 10:52 left.

"That was the turning point in the game," senior linebacker Torrance Marshall said. "When we got that score, we didn't look back."

Less than three minutes later, Josh Norman blocked a Husker punt, leading to a field goal and a 17-14 lead.

On OU's next possession, Heupel connected with Savage for 37 yards, setting up Norman's 8-yard touchdown run on an end around.

With 2:41 left in the first half, OU led, 24-14.

Neither offense scored in the second half. But OU's defense did.

Redshirt freshman cornerback Derrick Strait — whose wrong turn in the first quarter led to Nebraska's first score — might have sealed victory in the third quarter.

He intercepted Crouch's pass and returned it 32 yards for a touchdown and a 31-14 lead.

Almost 15 minutes later, Strait ended Nebraska's last realistic hope.

The Huskers had moved to the Sooner 23 when he stripped receiver Matt Davison after a short completion.

OU recovered the fumble. Nebraska never threatened again.

And that led to a final quarter that was anticlimactic for a national television audience, if not for the Sooners.

"It's the type of game people are going to talk about forever — "Where were you when the Sooners won that one?'" Burcham said. "It gives me goosebumps."

NEBRASKA	14	0	0	0	—	14
OKLAHOMA	0	24	7	10	—	31

OU ROMPS OVER BAYLOR

By George Schroeder
The Daily Oklahoman, Nov. 4, 2000

WACO, TEX. — Ho-hum.

In what might as well have been an off week, or maybe a scrimmage, Oklahoma easily defended its top ranking this afternoon, delivering a businesslike throttling of hapless Baylor.

After an October packed with drama, the matchup produced little suspense, but a lot of highlights. As 31,106 fans — more than half of them wearing crimson and cheering for the visitors — watched at Floyd Casey Stadium, the Sooners drubbed the Bears, 56-7.

"We came in here, we knew what we had to do," sophomore strong safety Roy Williams said, "and we did what we had to do."

Jump-started by J.T. Thatcher's 60-yard punt return for a touchdown, Oklahoma (8-0, 5-0 in the Big 12) led, 28-0, after one quarter and 42-0 at halftime. And, in a scene reminiscent of the Sooners of yesteryear, senior quarterback Josh Heupel and several other starters watched the second half from the sidelines without shoulder pads or helmets.

"It's been a while, probably since junior college," Heupel said of his second-half spectator's status. "But it was good to get everybody in."

Heupel was 21-of-29 for 313 yards and three touchdowns — plenty good enough to remain the front-runner for the Heisman Trophy. And OU remains in the driver's seat for the national championship.

The victory sets up a showdown Saturday at No. 24 Texas A&M that coach Bob Stoops called more important than OU's wins over Texas, Kansas State and Nebraska. The Aggies (7-2, 5-1 in the Big 12) got past Oklahoma State, 21-16, today in Stillwater.

"We're anxious to go down there and play," Stoops said. "We realize they'll be wild and waiting for us, but we look forward to the challenge."

OU (8-0, 5-0 in the Big 12) piled up 516 yards and 30 first downs and held Baylor (2-7, 0-6) to 94 total yards — a 1.6-yards-per-play average — and seven first downs.

Two weeks ago, then-No. 1 Nebraska held the Bears to 84 yards in a 59-0 win. But Baylor coach Kevin Steele, a former Nebraska assistant, was impressed with OU.

"I haven't seen a team ... that is better," Steele said.

True to form, the Sooners weren't satisfied.

"You want to be perfect," said sophomore receiver Curtis Fagan, who tied a school record with three touchdown catches, a feat unmatched since 1950. "People say no one can be perfect, but you want to be perfect."

For most of the first half, the Sooners were pretty close.

The halftime statistics told the story — and might have dictated second-half policy. Before joining the Sooners in the locker room, OU assistant coaches Chuck Long and Steve Spurrier Jr. held the press box elevator for a moment to grab a stat sheet.

Here's what they found: OU had 372 total yards at the half. Baylor had 46 yards on 31 plays.

And don't forget Heupel's numbers.

"He's probably the best quarterback I've ever faced," Baylor senior cornerback Daniel Wilturner said.

Said Stoops: "This may have been his best game. He threw some balls where guys were covered very well, and he was still able to put the ball just out of (the defender's) reach."

When the Sooners returned to the field for the second half, Heupel's shoulder pads remained in the locker room. But Stoops said the decision to bench Heupel was made based on the score, not the quarterback's statistics.

"We felt it was time to rest him," Stoops said.

Heupel's exit gave backup Nate Hybl his most extensive playing time of the season.

Hybl stuttered early — Odell James picked off a shovel pass and returned it 18 yards for Baylor's only score — but threw touchdown passes of 36 and 31 yards to Fagan and Antwone Savage, respectively.

The second half featured plenty of reserves, as well. Freshman linebackers Teddy Lehman and Jimmy Wilkerson played. All 11 offensive lineman played. Patrick Fletcher made a cameo appearance at wide receiver and was one of four quarterbacks to play.

"You like to see that," Stoops said. "That tells you the future of the program is coming, and you're building some depth ... . It was satisfying to see our second- and third-team guys on the field running around and playing well."

The only real discordant note came midway through the third quarter, when Thatcher injured his right knee while defending a pass. But Thatcher returned for the last few series and said later he was fine.

As expected, the rout was quickly on. OU's first possession stalled after one first down. But after the defense stuffed Baylor, Thatcher gathered Adam Stiles' punt at the OU 40, bolted up the middle and through a couple of Baylor arms, then cut around Antwone

Savage's block on Stiles and jogged into the end zone.

With 11:03 left in the first quarter, OU led, 7-0.

"That got us ready to go," Thatcher said. "It sparked everybody on the sidelines."

Led by Heupel and the Sooner receivers, OU scored touchdowns on its next four possessions. Heupel sneaked 4 yards for a TD, then hit Fagan for scores of 9 and 43 yards.

It wasn't always as pretty as the statistics. Several of Heupel's early passes were tipped, then grabbed by receivers. And Wilturner dropped an interception he almost certainly would have returned for a touchdown.

But there were stellar throws, like the 39-yard dart to fullback Seth Littrell for OU's sixth and final touchdown of the first half.

"Josh was his usual exceptional self," Stoops said. "There were some great catches ... . Josh put the ball where only they could make the catch. It's something to watch."

OKLAHOMA	28	14	14	0	—	56
BAYLOR	0	0	7	0	—	7

—— ᕰᑌ ——

BIG PLAYS GIVE SOONERS WIN OVER A&M

By George Schroeder
The Daily Oklahoman, Nov. 11, 2000

COLLEGE STATION, TEX. — As he rumbled off the field, index finger extended in the unmistakable symbol that continues to describe Oklahoma football, Scott Kempenich dropped the first of many references to an old friend of the program.

"Don't forget the Sooner Magic, buddy!" the senior offensive lineman said, yelling to be heard above the din. "You can't forget the Sooner Magic!"

How else to describe OU's 35-31 victory today at Kyle Field? How else to explain how the top-ranked Sooners overcame their own mistakes, a determined bunch of Texas A&M Aggies and 87,188 12th men — a stadium record — and escaped with their undefeated record and conference and national title hopes intact?

OU remains on the inside track to the Big 12 Championship game — and from there, to the Orange Bowl.

But for most of a gray November afternoon, No. 23 Texas A&M seemed poised to pull the upset.

The Aggies laid a trap that included a raucous crowd, a deceptive defense and an opportunistic offense. And with help from the

Sooners, almost snapped it shut.

OU could have easily crumbled beneath an unprecedented number of mistakes, including three turnovers and a blocked punt that led to 24 points.

But trailing by two touchdowns in the third quarter, the Sooners rallied. Grabbed the lead on Torrance Marshall's 41-yard interception return. Twice squelched A&M bids to regain the lead — once stopping the Aggies on fourth down from the 4.

And then left Kyle Field with a sense of how things used to be, when a mysterious intangible often lifted the Sooners to improbable victories. With a sense of how things are once more.

"Here in the new millennium, it's Sooner Magic, again," junior receiver Josh Norman said.

Said sophomore receiver Andre Woolfolk: "I've always heard about it. We're starting to get a glimpse of it."

In eight previous victories, OU had not trailed at halftime. But today, two turnovers and a blocked punt turned into a 17-10 A&M lead at intermission.

And, when Josh Heupel threw his second interception early in the third quarter, the Aggies took advantage again. Ja'Mar Toombs' 1-yard run stretched the Aggies' lead to 24-10.

But 24 minutes remained. The Sooners said they weren't overly concerned.

"No one's head was down," offensive coordinator Mark Mangino said. "Some of those kids were over there smiling and winking at each other, because they felt like, 'Hey, we'll get these guys.' "

Soon enough, the momentum began to turn. The Sooners were stymied in the first half by A&M's ever-shifting defensive schemes — mostly soft zone coverages that involved seven and eight defenders.

"They pulled out all the stops," Mangino said. "They did everything they could to try to stop us."

And did, up to a point. In the second half, OU took advantage of the soft coverage. The Sooners had 6 yards on eight rushing attempts in the first half, but managed 110 second-half yards on 20 carries.

"That's what got us back on track," Mangino said.

Heupel rebounded from the interceptions to lead OU on three scoring drives. That means Heupel's Heisman hopes remain alive. He completed 28 of 42 passes for 263 yards and rushed for 26 yards, including several crucial scrambles.

"I don't know what else anyone was looking for, the guy just finds a way to win," OU coach Bob Stoops said. "He's undefeated, we're undefeated and in the driver's seat of the Big 12 South. I don't think there's any question Josh has to be the leading candidate."

Fourteen seconds into the fourth quarter, OU pulled within three points, 24-21, on Quentin Griffin's 21-yard run and a two-point conversion.

But A&M rolled 80 yards in seven plays to stretch the lead to 10. A&M quarterback Mark Farris connected with receiver Robert Ferguson for 30 yards, and Toombs bulled the final 27 yards, dragging three defenders into the end zone.

"That's embarrassing," co-defensive coordinator Brent Venables said. "But we knew we had a chance to get back on the field and redeem ourselves."

First, the offense did its part.

OU answered with a 15-play, 77-yard drive. Heupel completed 6 of 7 passes and twice scrambled for 9 yards, the second time on third-and-seven to set up Griffin's 2-yard touchdown run that pulled OU to within 31-28 with 7:43 left.

And 25 seconds later, the Sooners led.

After the kickoff, Farris dropped back and threw for receiver Greg Porter on a route over the middle. Marshall recognized the pattern, picked off the pass and raced for the score.

It wasn't over. OU had to survive two more A&M possessions — including one that died at the OU 4, with a fourth-down incompletion near the goal line.

Helped by two costly penalties, the Aggies moved to a first down at the 10. But on fourth and goal from the 4, Farris' slant pass was behind receiver Chris Taylor; Ontei Jones may have gotten a hand on it.

"We were fortunate," co-defensive coordinator Brent Venables said. "It was a bad pass."

OU couldn't manage a first down and had to punt. But finally, with 36 seconds left, two Sooners stopped Porter 5 yards short on fourth and 20. One quick kneel later, OU was 9-0.

And the Sooners left town thinking about that mysterious intangible.

"Hopefully," Heupel said, "we've got a lot more magic left in the bag."

OKLAHOMA	3	7	3	22	—	35
TEXAS A&M	7	10	7	7	—	33

_____ OU _____

OU STRUGGLES BUT WINS BIG 12 SOUTH

By George Schroeder
The Daily Oklahoman, Nov. 18, 2000

NORMAN — The fans rained more oranges onto Owen Field on today, celebrating Oklahoma's latest achievement. But you'll have to pardon the Sooners if they didn't join the party.

With a 27-13 victory over Texas Tech, top-ranked OU wrapped up the Big 12 South and a trip to the conference championship game. But after a lackluster performance, the Sooners didn't feel much like celebrating.

"We're happy we're Big 12 South champions," sophomore strong safety Roy Williams said. "But until we do better, we're not going to be happy with our performance."

As 75,364 fans watched, the Sooners won despite four turnovers, two blocked kicks, 11 penalties and their lowest point total of the season. And the game wasn't decided until Quentin Griffin's touchdown with 1:53 left.

The victory, which more closely resembled those of September than the big wins in October, left the Sooners unsatisfied.

"I'm a little mad. Last week, we did the same thing," OU coach Bob Stoops said, referring to the Sooners' 35-31 victory at Texas A&M. "We're going to get after it in practice come Monday. We're not playing our best."

Still, the Sooners locked up their first division title. OU (10-0, 7-0 in the Big 12) will face No. 9 Kansas State in the Big 12 championship game on Dec. 2 at Kansas City's Arrowhead Stadium.

With a win next week at Oklahoma State, OU can finish the regular season undefeated for the first time since 1987. OU's national championship hopes remain intact. But the Sooners realize they'll have to improve to achieve that goal.

"We need to get better," said senior quarterback Josh Heupel, whose Heisman hopes might have taken a hit, "or we're going to trip up."

The game's outcome never seemed in doubt. But after OU led 21-3 in the third quarter, Tech closed within eight points with a fourth-quarter touchdown.

It took a 12-play, 71-yard drive capped by Griffin's score to put the pesky Red Raiders away.

"That showed a lot of character and toughness," coach Bob Stoops said.

Senior center Bubba Burcham said the preceding touchdown, which came on Tech quarterback Kliff Kingsbury's 15-yard pass to Tim Baker, served as a "wake-up, slap in the face."

OU's offense accounted for only three touchdowns and 384 yards, the second-lowest output this season.

Offensive coordinator Mark Mangino said he foresaw trouble last week, when practices, according to Burcham, were "dull and flat." And the Sooners played like it today.

"We were waiting around expecting something to happen instead of making it happen," Burcham said.

OU led, 14-3, at halftime despite running just 24 plays. One touchdown came on J.T. Thatcher's 85-yard interception return.

The Sooners' struggles might have been because of Tech's near-mirror-image attack. Both offenses were implemented by Tech coach Mike Leach, who was OU's offensive coordinator last year.

"I knew it would be difficult for both offenses, because the defenses see them day in and day out and just jump on the plays," Stoops said.

But the Sooners blamed themselves for plenty of troubles,

including dropped passes

"It was our ineptitude," Mangino said. "Any problems we had were caused by us."

Stoops agreed.

"Turnovers, dropping the ball, penalties, blocked kicks, those kinds of things you can't have," Stoops said. "We need to get some work done this week if we're going to continue to push like we want to."

Tech finished with 330 yards. Kingsbury completed 41 of 61 passes for 295 yards and a touchdown, but threw two interceptions. The Red Raiders controlled the clock, but struggled to score.

"Defense saved our butts all game long," OU senior offensive tackle Scott Kempenich said.

Heupel completed 24 of 38 passes for a season-low 248 yards and a touchdown, but threw two interceptions.

"We didn't have any tempo or rhythm," Heupel said.

But on the clinching fourth-quarter drive, Heupel completed 7 of 8 passes. That included a 15-yard, third-down connection with senior tight end Matt Anderson to set up Griffin's touchdown.

The pass off a bootleg was suggested by Heupel during a time-out.

"They're real consistent. They don't have any blatant weakness," Leach said. "They just keep coming every time. They just beat you."

But the Sooners aren't happy with the way they beat Tech.

"We're never going to get into a position where we don't appreciate a good win," Stoops said.

But a few moments later, he had another thought.

"It's still not good," he said. "Not for us."

TEXAS TECH	0	3	0	10	—	13
OKLAHOMA	7	7	7	6	—	27

SOONERS DODGE COWBOYS AMBUSH

By Bob Hersom
The Daily Oklahoman, Nov. 25, 2000

S TILLWATER — For an entire football season, the questions were: "What's wrong with Oklahoma State?" and "How about those Sooners?"

When that regular season ended Saturday, the questions were: "What's wrong with Oklahoma?" and "How about those Cowboys?"

And Oklahoma won.

The No. 1-ranked Sooners, favored by 25 points, edged the inspired Cowboys 12-7 in Bob Simmons' final game as the OSU head coach.

OU finished the regular season as major college football's only unbeaten (11-0) team, but didn't look nearly that good, at least on offense.

OSU finished a 3-8 regular season, but didn't looked nearly that bad, at least on defense.

While the Cowboys' season is over, the Sooners' remarkable campaign continues Saturday night in Kansas City, when OU plays 8th-ranked Kansas State for the Big 12 championship.

The Bedlam battle boiled down to OSU's final possession. The Cowboys, down 12-7, earned a first-and-goal at the OU 10 with 5:14

left. They eventually reached the OU 7, but the threat ended on two straight incompletions from the Sooners' 12.

OU quarterback Josh Heupel's Heisman Trophy hopes may have gone south (to Florida State's Chris Weinke) in this game that was nationally televised by Fox SportsNet.

Heupel, who had been fifth in NCAA total offense, completed only 16 of 39 passes for 154 yards. He threw two interceptions for the third straight week, and Cowboys dropped two other interceptions — one on OU's only touchdown drive of the day.

Other than four shovel passes for 51 yards, Heupel was a wind-chilled 12 of 35 for 103 yards.

The OU offense, which had been second in the nation in scoring, mustered only 10 points (the defense scored a safety) and 309 yards. The Sooners had been averaging 42.9 points and 452.3 yards (ninth nationally) a game.

The Sooners' point total is their lowest since a 29-0 loss at Texas A&M three years ago. OU's fewest points in coach Bob Stoops' two seasons had been 24 last year at Colorado.

Most of OU's offense was produced by tailback Quentin Griffin, who had 174 yards on runs and receptions. The Sooner dynamo was the game's leading rusher with 115 yards on 21 carries, and he also caught five passes for 59 yards.

Backup tailback Tatum Bell scored OSU's lone touchdown on a 60-yard run and finished with 90 yards on eight carries. Other than Bell's 60-yarder, the Pokes punched out only 113 yards on 37 carries.

Aso Pogi, OSU's redshirt freshman quarterback, seemed better than 9-for-20 for 102 yards, plus two interceptions. He also rushed for 42 yards and was never sacked.

OSU took the opening kickoff and drove 40 yards in six plays. The drive stalled at the OU 40, but Scott Elder's pooch punt was downed at OU's 1-yard line.

OU answered with a 99-yard touchdown drive, in which Griffin totaled 66 yards on runs and receptions. The march ended when split end Curtis Fagan caught his seventh TD pass, an OU record, from Heupel.

The Cowboys moved 50 yards to the OU 30, but they failed on fourth-and-one when Jamaal Fobbs was dropped for a two-yard loss by strong safety Roy Williams.

After an OU punt, OSU drove 49 yards to the OU 41, but the drive stopped when Sooner free safety J.T. Thatcher hatched his eighth pass interception of the year, tying an OU record.

Thatcher zigged and zagged and leapfrogged his way for a 35-yard interception return, to the OSU 33. Five snaps later, the Sooners settled for Duncan's 39-yard field goal.

After a pair of punts, OU's defense scored the final points of the half. Linebacker Rocky Calmus was credited with a sack and OU got a safety when Pogi was hurried into an intentional grounding call from the end zone.

OU led, 12-0, with 3:10 left in the first half. The rest of the second quarter continued the comedy of errors, as Heupel threw an interception, then Pogi threw an interception, then Heupel threw another interception before Pogi took a knee to end the half.

In the opening half, OU scored a touchdown, kicked a field goal, punted twice and threw two interceptions. OSU was even less productive, as the Cowboys failed on a fourth down, punted twice, threw two interceptions and gave up a safety.

The offensive scoreboard at halftime was OU 10, OSU minus-2.

After five punts filled the first nine minutes of the third quarter, OSU tailback Bell burst through left tackle for a 60-yard touchdown run.

The longest run and first TD of Bell's career cut OU's lead to 12-7 with 5:41 left in the third quarter.

In the fourth quarter, OU's Duncan was wide right on a 45-yard field goal try at 14:13, and OSU's final series ended at the OU 12 with 3:15 to play.

OKLAHOMA	7	5	0	0	—	12
OKLAHOMA ST.	0	0	7	0	—	7

ORANGE BOWL NEXT STOP FOR NO. 1 SOONERS

By George Schroeder
The Daily Oklahoman, Dec. 2, 2000

KANSAS CITY — Less than two minutes remained before the first oranges fell to the Arrowhead Stadium turf. And it wasn't because Oklahoma fans were worried about legal repercussions. They could hardly have tossed the fruit earlier. And as it turns out, they were a few seconds premature.

OU's 27-24 victory over Kansas State tonight wasn't clinched until Damian Mackey recovered an onside kick with 5 seconds left on the Arrowhead Stadium scoreboard.

As 79,655 fans watched in frigid temperatures, top-ranked OU broke away from a 17-17 tie with 10 fourth-quarter points, then outlasted No. 8 Kansas State to win the Big 12 Championship.

"This win just describes our season," OU coach Bob Stoops said. "With all of the pressure of being No. 1, we were still able to come through in the end."

The Sooners will play for their seventh national title on Jan. 3 in the Orange Bowl. Their opponent will be announced today, but it's almost certain to be No. 3 Florida State, which will probably be No. 2 in the Bowl Championship Series rankings.

"Now, we've got a whole month to think about it," Stoops said of the Sooners' impending shot at history. "I can't wait. We have a great history with the Orange Bowl, and I hope that excellent history continues."

OU won its 37th conference championship and first since 1987. That's also the last time OU visited the Orange Bowl, and the last time OU had a shot at the national championship.

OU notched its 12th victory — an unprecedented accomplishment in a program filled with tradition — and its second win this season over Kansas State (9-3).

The Sooners won the first meeting 41-31 on Oct. 14 at Manhattan, Kan., a game wasn't as close as the final score.

The rematch was never anything but close until late. But as in every other game in a season of perfection, the Sooners made the big plays.

"We just do enough to win," quarterback Josh Heupel said.

Said Kansas State coach Bill Snyder: "Oklahoma just played better than us. They deserved it."

Heupel's 17-yard touchdown toss to Andre Woolfolk on the second play of the fourth quarter gave OU a 24-17 lead. And after OU grabbed a 10-point lead on Tim Duncan's 46-yard field goal with 1:25 left, the Wildcats made things interesting with a 16-yard touchdown toss from Jonathan Beasley to Quincy Morgan with 6 seconds left.

Heupel completed 24 of a season-high 44 passes — for 220 yards. He threw three interceptions, but offset that with two touchdowns and led OU on three second-half scoring drives. His 17-yard touchdown pass to Andre Woolfolk with 14:24 left in the fourth quarter gave OU a lead it never relinquished.

But the game wasn't sealed until Duncan's season-long field goal knuckled through the uprights with 1:25 left. The Sooners faced fourth and 3 at the Kansas State 27.

Most of the credit for the victory should go to OU's defense, which held Kansas State's offense to 17 points — one touchdown came on a punt return — and 239 yards. The Sooners harassed Wildcat quarterback Jonathan Beasley into a 12-for-28, 106-yard performance and held the Wildcats to 133 yards rushing.

"Our defense may have been the story of the game," Stoops said. "What we did all day was pretty special."

Said Beasley: "They did a great job stuffing what we were doing."

OU's offense managed only 85 yards at halftime, when the game was tied at 10, but began to move in the third quarter. And 115 of OU's 319 total yards came in the fourth quarter. The Sooners finished with 99 yards rushing; 76 yards came in the fourth quarter. Quentin Griffin had 87 yards on 13 carries; 52 came in the final quarter.

OU grabbed a 17-10 lead with its first sustained drive. The Sooners moved 69 yards in eight plays; Heupel scored from 7 yards out.

Heupel hit Trent Smith for 17 yards. Griffin faked a reverse, then raced 25 yards around left end. Two plays later, Heupel looked for a receiver, found the right half of the field empty and raced untouched for the score with 5:54 left in the third quarter.

A few moments later, the Wildcats tied the game on Tulsa Washington graduate Aaron Lockett's 58-yard punt return. Lockett grabbed Jeff Ferguson's line-drive punt on the run and bolted up the right hash for the touchdown, leaving Ferguson twisting in vain near the 20.

The Sooners answered early in the fourth quarter. Heupel led a nine-play, 79-yard drive keyed by perhaps the game's biggest play.

On the first play of the fourth quarter, OU faced fourth and 1 at the Kansas State 39. Heupel took the option left and pitched — high — to Griffin, who raced 22 yards to the 17.

"That was just some Oklahoma football of old," Stoops said. "We haven't forgotten totally about the option."

From there, Heupel found Woolfolk wide open on a post pattern, and OU led, 24-17, with 14:24 left in the game.

The Sooners put the game away with a nine-play, 59-yard drive for Duncan's field goal. Griffin had a 29-yard run on the same option play, and Heupel rushed five times for 20 yards.

KANSAS ST.	0	10	7	7	—	24
OKLAHOMA	3	7	7	10	—	27

STRONG DEFENSE, DUNCAN'S KICKS DEFEAT SEMINOLES

By George Schroeder
The Daily Oklahoman, Jan. 3, 2001

M IAMI — Josh Heupel and the offense brought Oklahoma to the brink of a national championship, a swarming Sooner defense brought home the trophy tonight. As 76,835 watched at Pro Player Stadium — and the nation watched on ABC — the Sooners reclaimed their place atop college football with a 13-2 Orange Bowl victory over heavily favored Florida State, which completed a season of perfection. It was also the completion of a remarkable rise. It is OU's seventh national championship, the first since the 1985 season.

But 25 months ago, a once-proud program was in shambles. When Bob Stoops was hired, the Sooners had just finished their third consecutive losing season. He has orchestrated a turnaround so rapid no crystal ball could have foretold.

Tonight, Stoops held aloft the crystal football that sits atop the Sears Trophy, which will soon join the other six national championship trophies in the Barry Switzer Center.

"I think now it's easy to say that Oklahoma is officially back," Stoops said.

Florida State, which was ranked No. 3 in The Associated Press and coaches' polls, entered the game as a 10-point favorite.

"There was no hoping about it," Stoops said. "We expected to win this game."

Victory came in the most improbable way. Stoops brought the forward pass to OU. But perhaps fitting his roots as a defensive coach, this game was won by a stifling defense that shut down and shut out the nation's top offense.

The Seminoles averaged 42.4 points and 549 yards during the regular season. Playing with Heisman Trophy winner Chris Weinke but without all-American receiver Snoop Minnis, the Seminoles managed 301 yards — 53 yards came on a final, futile drive.

"They had a lot of weapons. We had to stop them all," junior defensive end Cory Heinecke said. "As long as we played as a unit, we were going to be all right."

Florida State's only score came on a safety with 55 seconds left, when Ben Panter's snap sailed high over punter Jeff Ferguson's head. That score helped the Seminoles avoid their first shutout since 1988.

But the Sooners will probably count it, anyway. Florida State's best chance for an offensive score was a wobbly missed field goal in the second quarter.

"Are you kidding me?" Stoops said. "Everyone recognizes our defense still has the shutout. And they don't get shut out very often."

The Sooners mixed zone and man pass coverage and kept the Seminoles off-balance. Florida State had 27 rushing yards on 17 carries and converted one of 15 third-down attempts.

"We didn't play one defense we hadn't played all year," Stoops said. "We just mixed it up a little bit."

Said Florida State coach Bobby Bowden: "We simply could not get anything going against them. No consistency whatsoever."

OU took a 6-0 lead — manufactured on two field goals by Tim Duncan — into the fourth quarter. And then, midway through the final quarter, the defense delivered the crucial takeaway.

Backed near his own end zone, Weinke scrambled for an apparent first down. But junior linebacker Rocky Calmus popped the football loose. Strong safety Roy Williams recovered the fumble.

Two plays later, Quentin Griffin bolted untouched 10 yards for the clinching touchdown.

"Our players recognize the history of Oklahoma is about winning championships," Stoops said. "We already had six national championships. Now, we have seven. ... You can't say, 'Well, that was then, this is now.'

"This is Oklahoma football."

Weinke finished 25 of 51 for 274 yards, with two interceptions.

"We couldn't match up," Bowden said. "They stayed a step ahead of us all the way defensively."

Late in the game, Sooner fans chanted "Heupel Heisman!"

Playing against a rugged Seminole defense, Heupel didn't have that kind of performance. But after Weinke's pass was intercepted in the end zone with 11 seconds left, the Heisman runner-up took one final snap to run out the clock.

"Out of this season, this is absolutely what he wanted, to win the national championship," Stoops said. "Great leader. He got what he wanted, and that's what's most important."

OU's offense didn't produce much. OU managed 270 yards; Heupel completed 25 of 39 passes for 214 yards with one interception.

But the Sooners did enough. Duncan hit two of three field goals, connecting from 27 and 42 yards.

And Griffin delivered the dagger with that touchdown with 7:46 left.

The offense's most important production might have been controlling the football. OU held possession for 36:33 to Florida State's 23:27.

"We moved the ball and moved the clock," Stoops said.

Said co-defensive coordinator Brent Venables: "Our offense did a heck of a job controlling the clock. That was a big, big factor."

But this was the defense's night. Pick a hero. Just make sure he's a defender.

| FLORIDA STATE | 0 | 0 | 0 | 2 | — | 2 |
| OKLAHOMA | 3 | 0 | 3 | 7 | — | 13 |

STOOP'S TROPHY CASE

Big 12 Champions – 2000

National Champions – 2000

Big 12 Coach of the Year – 1999, 2000

*Walter Camp Football Foundation
Coach of the Year – 2000*

*The Associated Press
National Coach of the Year – 2000*

*American Football Coaches Association
Coach of the Year – 2000*

Eddie Robinson/FWAA Coach of the Year – 2000

Bear Bryant Coach of the Year – 2000